O CLAP YOUR HANDS

A MUSICAL TOUR OF SACRED CHORAL WORKS

GORDON GILES

AUTHOR OF *O Come Emmanuel*

ACCOMPANYING CD SUNG BY

Gloriæ Dei Cantores • www.gdcchoir.org

PARACLETE PRESS
Brewster, Massachusetts

O Clap Your Hands: A Musical Tour of Sacred Choral Works

2008 First Printing

Copyright © 2008 by Gordon Giles

ISBN: 978-1-55725-567-9

Unless otherwise noted all scriptural references are taken from the *New Revised Standard Version,* copyright 1989, 1995 by the Division of Christian Education of the National Council of Churches of Christ in the United States of America. Used by permission. All rights reserved.

Scripture references marked KJV are taken from the *King James Version* of the Bible.

Library of Congress Cataloging-in-Publication Data

Giles, Gordon, 1966-
    O clap your hands : a musical tour of sacred choral works / Gordon Giles.
    p. cm.
    ISBN-13: 978-1-55725-567-9
    1. Hymns—History and criticism. 2. Church music. I. Title.
    BV315.G55 2008
    264'.23—dc22
                                    2008000174

10 9 8 7 6 5 4 3 2 1

Published by Paraclete Press
Brewster, Massachusetts
www.paracletepress.com

Printed in the United States of America

Church-musick

Sweetest of sweets, I thank you: when displeasure
*   Did through my bodie wound my minde,*
You took me thence, and in your house of pleasure
*   A daintie lodging me assign'd.*

Now I in you without a bodie move,
*   Rising and falling with your wings:*
We both together sweetly live and love,
*   Yet say sometimes, God help poore Kings.*

Comfort, I'le die; for if you poste from me,
*   Sure I shall do so, and much more:*
But if I travell in your companie,
*   You know the way to heaven's doore.*

from *The Temple*, 1633, George Herbert (1593–1633)

Contents

A Four-Session Group Study of *O Clap Your Hands*

How This Book Might Be Used

The compact disc in the sleeve of this book contains thirty tracks by Gloriæ Dei Cantores, arranged in the same order as the chapters of the book. There is no "correct" way to listen to the music and to read the text; I hope you will find a way that is helpful and inspiring to you. My only intention is the obvious one, which is that the music be listened to and the meditation read in reasonably close proximity. If you want to be methodical, you can listen to the tracks consecutively, reading the accompanying reflections as you go. You might do this daily (in which case, you have precisely a whole month's worth, if you select April, June, September, or November). This book can form a month of devotions, if you wish. But you will not be impoverished if you read and listen at whatever pace suits you. There is a logical order to the chapters, in that there is a seasonal progression in the central chapters, and five consecutive chapters on the movements of the Mass. This format makes sense if the chapters are read in the proper order. However, each chapter is intended to stand alone. I hope, therefore, that the book will also be valuable to dip into when time or mood permits. You can, of course, listen to the CD in your car as a fine mixed collection of choral music, and then read the book before you go to sleep at night.

Personal Devotion

For those who like to use the book and CD as a devotional aid for personal quiet time, you might like to try this approach:

Find somewhere comfortable to sit, well lit and quiet. Make sure your CD player can be programmed to only play one track, and that you can use the remote control, or reach the buttons on the player without having to get up. Listen to the music all the way through once. If you wish to listen to it again, feel free to do so. Then read the reflection, at whatever pace suits you. If you want to listen to all or part of the piece again because of what you are reading, go ahead. When you have finished the reflection, keep silent for a little while and then pray the prayer, either in your head or aloud. Then listen to the whole piece through one final time. This exercise could take anywhere from fifteen to thirty minutes, depending on the piece and your desire for time with God. Try not to just spend time with the music and the words, but see them as opening a door somewhere else, where I hope and pray our Lord might reveal something to you.

Small Group Devotion

Small groups can approach this book basically the same as above. However, it is important to allow time for everyone to read at their own pace, or have someone read the text aloud. You will need to decide how often to play the piece. It might be simplest to play it at the beginning and again at the end. Other prayers may be used to conclude each session, and a corporate saying of the Lord's Prayer would also be appropriate. I would recommend not doing more than one chapter at a time, but if you do, remember to leave space between chapters if you are going to do several in one day.

Group Study Course

It is also possible to use the material in this book for a Group Discussion, meeting on four occasions, weekly, monthly, or whenever. Material and questions for leading and following such a course will be found at the end of the book.

However you use this book and CD, may they be a blessing to you, and "whatever you do, do everything for the glory of God" (1 Corinthians 10:31).

Introduction

St. Augustine of Hippo said that anyone who sings, prays twice. Anyone who sings, even sixteen centuries later, is bound to agree with him. Yet so much has changed musically since then that we might be inclined to say that Augustine was more right than he might have imagined. He would have had no insight into what we, in postmedieval Western civilization, call harmony and counterpoint, tempered tonality and a range of instrumentation and virtuosity that grows as every new style and talent is born.

I am not suggesting that everyone who sings or plays music is in some way worshiping God. Worship is a conscious act, in which one encounters our heavenly Father through Christ and in the power of the Spirit. Singing glorifies God if, and only if, we engage with and own the words, which are the poetry of praise. The best hymns enable us in each of our spiritual treasuries to have some hymns that we love to sing, and that, in some way, speak to us and enable us to speak to God. These hymns exemplify the action of the Holy Sprit, who is both the enabler and the object of praise. As we lift our voices to God in song, we are ourselves uplifted and the encounter becomes two-directional. We sing to God and the Spirit sings with us, bearing us up to the throne of grace.

Participating in Music

Music can be enjoyed and participated in, in various ways. Millions of people enjoy listening to recordings of music, whether it is what we call "classical" music, "pop" music, or other genres. The mere act of listening to music involves us in the sound world of the composer and brings us into a realm where our minds and our spirits can be engaged, soothed, or aroused. Listening to music is contrasted with "hearing" music, which is what happens when we play it as background music. The Muzak Corporation invented a particular form of musical background, the name of which has become synonymous with music that is heard, not listened to. Music, properly speaking, is to be listened to and requires the attention of our minds and spirits. The listener therefore is a crucial member of the trio that is needed for all performances: composer, performer, and listener. In a church service, the listener—that is, one who does not perform, but who partakes in the pews so to speak—is as significant as those who sing or play, for the singing and playing is done for their benefit. In this way, the whole congregation is involved when a group sings or plays in worship.

Yet music, even when played alone, is a participatory activity. When playing or singing a solo, the performer is relating to the composer: not the person who died years ago, or who lives miles away, but the composer-in-the-work. Like other art forms, music is laden with intention. Every note composed is deliberate; choices have been made, including the ultimate choice to share the music—*this* music—with the world. Thus when a performer takes up a sheet of music, a conversation begins, and any prospect of loneliness or alienation is banished. (Such a positive engagement does not always occur: not all relationships work the first time, if at all.)

Some people pray when playing music alone, and complete immersion in the music and the removal of everything else can open the way for inspiration, communion, or even hearing the voice of God. This very possibility frightened early church leaders who believed music to be highly dangerous. Practiced by sorcerers and dancers and other pagans, they feared its power to entrance and enable the mind to be corrupted if emptied of godly thoughts!

If singing alone can bring inspiration and delight, how much more can shared music bring! Hymn singing and school songs have as their main strength communality of feeling and common purpose, whether it be in search of divine blessing or of a sporting victory. Some people suggest that singing at sports games, especially in Europe, has displaced hymn singing, but hymn singing has by no means died out. The two activities have something in common:

the unificatory ability of song, and the emotional stimulation of shared music. Augustine felt that communal singing was a force to be reckoned with. Yet he did not know about piano duets, string quartets, nor most importantly of all, church choirs.

Anyone who plays or sings chamber music will know firsthand the deep delight coming from the blend of work and pleasure that a small ensemble creates. Chamber music needs no audience; musicians sometimes get together simply to play or sing. They enjoy each other's company at the musical level, and those who have played together over many years form a kind of musical family unit that is both intimate and mutual. The individual members of a string quartet, for example, need not be best friends, but when they take up their bows they become different people, tied by the strings of their instruments.

If solo performance is like hitting a ball against a wall, and chamber music is like mixed doubles, then orchestral playing is like the big game. While music is not generally competitive, it shares with sports the challenge, joy, and benefit of teamwork. A football team that cannot work together will lose. An orchestra that cannot work together will fall apart. Musicians must listen to one another as they play, just as athletes must watch one another and the ball. These are not only skills of awareness, they are skills of relationship, and they are needed and cherished in churches too. Next time you are in church, look around at those with you: are they OK? Is some part of the liturgy, the music, or the Word touching them? Who has had a bad week? The measure of a welcoming church community is "do they care about each other?" Do they even know each other well enough to recognize a person in need?

Musical Fellowship and Spiritual Teamwork

When a group is working toward a common spiritual cause or purpose, such as leading worship or running a soup kitchen, there is a kind of "spiritual teamwork" involved. The bond that exists in the group is not merely practical, but also spiritual. Corporate music making is like this too, and enables us to team up, not only with each other, but also with the Holy Spirit, who joins our praise. Moreover, there is true fellowship in musical teamwork that is devoted to God. Members of choirs know that there is something very special about making music together, and something extra special about doing it for God, who welcomes our best efforts.

Fellowship is a word often bandied about, usually in a positive sense, but there is a risk of it becoming meaningless. What is fellowship? For some it consists simply in Christians socializing together. For others it is corporate worship, or the time of refreshment afterward. A "time of fellowship" can mean so many different things nowadays that if one is invited to participate one will not know what will come to pass! But whatever "fellowship" denotes, it centers on the common purpose and faith of those sharing it, and the sharing of it is probably more important than the "it," if you see what I mean. Thus we can truly say that members of the choir, or the music group, are in fellowship with one another, not only when they have their parties or outings or postrehearsal refreshments, but especially when they stand as one and sing to the Lord. This is spiritual teamwork, musical fellowship, and it makes church music special and holy.

Musical Offering

Critiquing music performed in church can undermine the spiritual dimension of what is being offered. Musical performance involves skill, practice, interpretation, and courage, stress, perfectionism, and sometimes even rivalry. It is both appropriate and easy to say that such attitudes are unfitting or unnecessary, but they do occur from time to time in church settings. Human beings are complex, and our motivations and desires are not always simple. The spiritual teamwork of musical worship can be affected by the stress and strain that affect all musical performers. While ecclesiastical performance can lead to tremendous spiritual teamwork, the pressure of the performance can also undermine unity.

A way to understand and alleviate this potential difficulty is to distinguish between a performance in a concert hall, which is generally an offering to the audience, and a performance during worship, which is an offering to God in which both performers and congregation partake. It could be said that church music is not performed at all, but is offered. Performance is what players do with their instruments when they produce a string of noises in accordance with some instructions issued by a composer and receive applause afterward. To some extent this definition holds true in worship (whether people applaud or not), but performance of music in a religious context is subtly different. With the exception of a recent trend to applaud an organist after the postlude (an appreciative gesture that I suspect relates to their conduct of the whole service and the fact that it prevents chatter immediately after the service), applause for music during a service is rare in many churches.

Perhaps we should applaud our church musicians more often, but we do not because the reason is and always has been that the performance of music in church is somehow different. It is not "performed" as at some fair or concert, but *offered*. This sense of offering our music, and ourselves through it, typifies what happens in church and distinguishes it from what happens in a concert. That is why, during Holy Week, one might attend a concert in a local church and hear Lotti's *Crucifixus* sung beautifully, and join in the riotous applause that follows. A few days later on Good Friday, the same choir might sing the same composition in the same building and the congregation will not clap but weep. The audience applauds, but the congregation partakes, welcomed by the musicians into the fellowship of worship. This participation goes beyond performance; it is almost a form of communion: a participation in something that transcends mere performance.

For when the choir sings in worship, we are all in the choir. Not all in the congregation sing the anthem, but all are involved. All are connected in spirit if not in voice. As the body of Christ joined in praise together, we are one, and even if only some of our members actually sing with their mouths and lungs, we all sing with our souls. That is and always has been the ultimate purpose of ecclesiastical music.

Spiritual Gifts

In the First Letter to the Corinthians, St. Paul explains the purpose and quality of what we have come to call "spiritual gifts." The examples of spiritual gifts that he gives is not an exhaustive list, and while we should be in no doubt about the gifts he does mention, we might well consider whether other gifts that we value, music among them, can now be considered as spiritual gifts too. It seems obvious that musical ability, like any artistic talent or practical skill, is a gift bestowed by God, for which he can and should be praised, and that may be used in his service. But can we consider music to be a "spiritual gift"?

St. Paul's teaching on spiritual gifts is worth quoting at length here:

> *Now there are varieties of gifts, but the same Spirit; and there are varieties of services, but the same Lord; and there are varieties of activities, but it is the same God who activates all of them in everyone. To each is given the manifestation of the Spirit for the common good. To one is given through the Spirit the utterance of wisdom, and to another the utterance of knowledge according to the same Spirit, to another faith by the same Spirit, to another gifts of healing by the one Spirit, to another the working of miracles, to another prophecy, to another the discernment of spirits, to another various kinds of tongues, to another the interpretation of tongues. All these are activated by one and the same Spirit, who allots to each one individually just as the Spirit chooses. For just as the body is one and has many members, and all*

*the members of the body, though many, are one body, so
it is with Christ. For in the one Spirit we were all baptized
into one body—Jews or Greeks, slaves or free—and we
were all made to drink of one Spirit. . . .*

*. . . God has so arranged the body, giving the greater honor
to the inferior member, that there may be no dissension
within the body, but the members may have the same care
for one another. If one member suffers, all suffer together
with it; if one member is honored, all rejoice together
with it. Now you are the body of Christ and individually
members of it. And God has appointed in the church first
apostles, second prophets, third teachers; then deeds of
power, then gifts of healing, forms of assistance, forms of
leadership, various kinds of tongues. Are all apostles? Are
all prophets? Are all teachers? Do all work miracles? Do
all possess gifts of healing? Do all speak in tongues? Do all
interpret? But strive for the greater gifts. And I will show
you a still more excellent way.*
(1 Corinthians 12:4–13, 24–31)

Paul's articulation of spiritual gifts is clear enough: God
blesses us in different ways, with different talents. The diversity
we find at the creation of the world when different creatures are
made is also present in the varying natures of the human race, the
species made in the image of God. Indeed, our diversity may well
reflect the multifaceted dimension of God, for no single human
being has or could have all the features of God, because such
diversity cannot be present in any being who is not divine. Thus,
as Paul suggests, there is something both natural and divine in our
built-in diversity. We are good at different things, and a Christian
community cherishes and relishes the prospect of diversity.

The Corinthian community to whom Paul was writing had
given him headaches over the years, so that at least five letters were

exchanged, the exact order of which is still under debate. We do not have the responses that the Corinthian church leaders sent Paul, but he evidently did receive some feedback, because 1 and 2 Corinthians clearly refer to issues they raise. The distribution and relative value of spiritual gifts was such an issue that Paul felt the need to address them. At the time, more "showy" spiritual practices involving strange utterances and bodily convulsions were held in great regard in pagan society, whereas quieter piety and less colorful behavior were seen as second division gifts, if gifts at all. Paul sets them right, and leaves us with a description that has inspired the church ever since and that leads him to describe the virtues of love, the "more excellent way"—a way that trumps a clanging gong and endures even beyond faith and hope.

Music in the Bible

Paul does not mention music as such, and in this he is not unique. In fact, when we consider how important music has been and still is to every society, it is quite remarkable how infrequently it is mentioned in the Bible. The history of Western culture, which is in large part a Christian history, has at its heart the history of Western music, which has literally accompanied the great events and cultural movements of the last millennium. So to us today, who know and love music, there is something unsatisfactory in the Bible's relative silence on the subject (or so it may seem). Because we know in our hearts how uplifting, praiseworthy, and praise-giving music can be, we need to feel that in using it in worship we are standing in a great tradition that is musical, spiritual, and biblical.

The Bible tells us that the first musician was Jubal (Genesis 4:21), who played both the lyre and the pipes (the name *Jubal* may be derived from the Hebrew word *ram*, suggesting he played a ram's horn, or *shofar*, a significant ancient instrument used in Jewish worship). Music accompanied or heralded battle, and sometimes women led singing and dancing. Miriam danced after the deliverance from Egypt (Exodus 15), and Deborah and Barak sang a victory song (Judges 5).

The Psalms were the hymnbook of the ancient Jews, particularly after the end of the Babylonian exile in the middle of the sixth century BC. Only one psalm is known to be from that period of exile: Psalm 137, "by the rivers of Babylon." The dating of the other psalms is uncertain and much debated, but some claim to be by King David, and some scholars see no reason to doubt their authenticity. It is nevertheless a mistake to assume that David wrote all the psalms personally. However, the association with David is strong and valid enough to give David a reputation in the Hebrew Bible as the archetypal musician, portrayed throughout history with a lyre or harp.

Once the temple was established at Jerusalem, professional musicians became necessary, and the women musicians and dancers were disenfranchised. At best, the people sang the responses to what the professional men intoned. There was no harmony as such, and everything was sung from memory. A singer's training took five years, but they may have been selected and partially trained in childhood. The music of the temple was a necessary feature of worship: without singing the sacrifice was not valid. Special settings were composed and sung at particular points in the liturgy, along with designated psalms. There is evidence that some of the psalm-singing would have involved the congregation at times. Individual psalms were sometimes headed with musical instructions, indicating either how it should be performed, indications of which tune to use, or guidelines as to the function of the particular psalm. As these headings may have originally been written on scrolls as marginal notes for music leaders, and then, as such, not always copied carefully, they have caused some confusion over the centuries and still appear in some Bibles. Of the many words appearing in this way, *selah* is probably the most well-known, being the most common. It is also the most enigmatic, but is probably an instruction to pause the singing, or insert a musical interlude in the midst of the psalm.

The music of the Jewish temple was sophisticated and was integral to the religion of the day, thus commanding effort, finances, and attention.

Music in Ancient Greek Culture

Meanwhile, the ancient Greeks were also exploring music, and two hundred years after the Jews returned to Israel from the exile, Plato (c. 428–347 BC) felt it necessary to point out that music could be dangerous because of its ability to take over the consciousness of listeners. His concern was mainly for the *aulos* and the *kithara*, ancestors of the flute and guitar respectively, and he banned the former from his ideal city-state or Republic. Plato's purpose was fundamentally religious. In *The Republic*, Plato claims that the *aulos* is linked to the satyr Marsyas, an evil being, whereas the lyre and kithara are the chosen instruments of Apollo, whom the Muses follow. These opinions formed the basis of the idea that music should serve the state religion, and so pipes were out (except for shepherds') and strings were in. Plato was also well aware of and sought to take advantage of the fact that music serves an educative purpose, and proposed that everyone in the community should "voice always one and the same sentiment in song, story and speech" (Laws ii, 664a). For Plato, therefore, music could be dangerous, but it also could be used to guide others in matters of politics and religion.

Music at the Crossroads

The contrast between Hebrew and Greek attitudes toward music is very important, for these two strands meet in the Middle East in the first century. Of course, music was by no means the most important issue that went into the melting pot of that time and place, but it is both symptomatic and indicative of wider concerns. The first Jewish Christians inherited the tradition of singing in worship, and the Gentile believers would have known other musical traditions associated with festivals and pagan rites. For new converts, worship without music would simply not have worked. The use of music may well have proved a unifying force where Gentile and Jewish Christians came together: it has been long known that music can break down divisions and differences and assist unity and fellowship. While we can only surmise this to some extent, we do know that singing in praise of God was in vogue when Jesus was born: the angels praised God and the shepherds heard them (Luke 2:13–14), and at the end of his earthly life, Jesus and the disciples sang a hymn together before going out to the Garden of Gethsemane (Mark 14:26), just as they would have done had they been at the synagogue. Paul commends hymn singing and music in the context of worship: "When you come together, each one has a hymn, a lesson, a revelation, a tongue, or an interpretation. Let all things be done for building up" (1 Corinthians 14:26). He also writes: " . . . be filled with the Spirit, as you sing psalms and hymns and spiritual songs among yourselves, singing and making melody to the Lord in your hearts, giving thanks to God the Father at all times and for everything in the name of our Lord Jesus Christ" (Ephesians 5:18–20, also Colossians 3:16). He also describes himself as being one who sings: "I will sing praise with the spirit, but I will sing praise with the mind also" (1 Corinthians 14:15b). Paul is not going to be manipulated by music or allow it to deprive him of reason.

The religious music with which the Jewish Christians were familiar would have been synagogical, whereby a cantor, rather than a choir, would lead. The cantor needed to be a good singer, well versed in Scripture, humble, and not wealthy (for then it was said his prayers would not come from his heart!).

There is no reason to suppose that music in worship was discouraged at this time, even if we have to look hard for signs of encouragement. But lurking in the background was the attitude of those who either were Greek or who had been influenced by that culture. Where music was seen as aligned with pagan religion, there was a problem, and it is extremely likely that the musical world of Corinth was beset with musicians who were involved in practices frowned upon by the early church, such as sorcery and idolatry. It is easy to conceive how music might serve the purposes of either activity. Equally annoying was the attitude of the Romans, the rulers of the Middle East, who believed that music was basically for entertainment. Both Greek and Roman attitudes confronted and influenced the ancient and reverential Jewish view on music in worship. Paul, when writing to the Greeks of Corinth, was writing to those who probably disagreed with his Jewish views, but neither of them would have thought of music as merely entertainment.

Music as a Spiritual Gift

When it comes to the passage from 1 Corinthians in which Paul extols the various spiritual gifts, equating them and giving them due attention, we might well wonder why he does not mention music. As we have seen, music was very important in Jewish culture and worship and must have been valued as a gift. One explanation for Paul's omitting it in his letter to Corinth was that it was too hot an issue. Or it was not an issue at all: they had not raised it, and Paul was not going to stir it by raising the difficulty that arose between Jewish and Greek cultures as to what music was for and how it should be employed to the glory of God. Can it be true that Paul, a Jew, "advanced in Judaism beyond many among my people of the same age, for I was far more zealous for the traditions of my ancestors" (Galatians 1:14) would not have had high regard for the role of music in worship?

Since before the time of Christ, we can detect seeds of ambivalence toward the use of music, and since Christ himself is not recorded as having made any significant comment about it, confusion about the merits and use of music in and outside church has persisted. Nowadays few doubt that music has power to lift our hearts and voices to God; that it can be a channel of grace, and a gift with which some, but not all, are blessed. Those who are blessed with musical talent can certainly offer it to God's glory:

many have done so over the centuries to the delight and comfort of countless others.

Paul's account of gifts points to a bigger picture in which all Christians, as members of the body of Christ, are called and blessed with the means to serve and worship God. Some are musicians, and while Paul would have seen some Greek or Roman musicians as dubious characters, their talent in itself was by no means evil, and, as with many things, they would need to reform their former pagan practices and convert the whole of their lives: a difficult but not impossible task. His reminder to the Ephesians would have served the Corinthians well too: "You were taught to put away your former way of life, your old self, corrupt and deluded by its lusts, and to be renewed in the spirit of your minds, and to clothe yourselves with the new self, created according to the likeness of God in true righteousness and holiness" (Ephesians 4:22–24). In some cases the Corinthians' licentiousness or pagan idolatry would have gone hand in hand with certain musical behavior, the singing of particular songs, or the playing of instruments for rituals or practices that Christianity, as presented by Paul to the Corinthians, frowned upon. It was not music itself that was a thorny issue, but that with which it was often associated could be.

It is also worth noting that given the appalling reputation that musicians had in Greek and Roman culture, it is remarkable that Paul is not recorded as singling them out for specific criticism. As late as the fourth century, John Chrysostom berated musicians as highly suspicious characters. Perhaps in response to those who had absorbed Platonist views into their Christian faith, *aulos* players were even refused baptism because they were generally associated with sorcery and sexual immorality.

Yet Paul, centuries earlier, had not condemned any musicians. More likely he preferred to condemn practices that he knew to be wrong, such as incest, lying, and sorcery, and praised those things that he knew to be valuable, such as speaking in tongues and prophecy. It also seems likely that prophecy and speaking in tongues are simply fine *examples* of spiritual gifts, and that there can be others, and today we would surely want to include music among them.

Music Becomes Acceptable

As we enter the medieval period, we find that after Augustine, music and musicians became much more acceptable. Inspired by Pythagorus (c. 580–c. 500 BC), the Christian philosopher Boethius (AD 480–c. 524) maintained that music reflected the order of creation, and thus its contemplation and use in worship should be encouraged. By this time, Augustine had lived and died, and we have already seen how positive he was about music's ability to aid devotion. He wrote:

> In the Psalms it says "O Sing to the Lord a new song; sing his praise in the assembly of the saints." We are urged to sing to the Lord a new song. It is a new person who sings a new song. A song is a joyful thing, and if we reflect more deeply, it is also a matter of love. Thus anyone who has learned how to love a new life will also have learned how to sing a new song. For the sake of the new song however, we need to be reminded what the nature of the new life is. Indeed a new person, a new song and the new covenant are all manifestations of the one kingdom: a new person will both sing a new song and belong to the new covenant. (Sermon 34.1)

Augustine, who had been brought up on Plato, was well aware of the power of music to arouse emotion, and believed that this same power could help people direct their devotions to God. How right he was!

Our Sacred Musical Inheritance

Since the Christianization of Europe and the subsequent fall of Rome, Christian music has never looked back. For many, Western music has its origins in the music of the Jewish temple, the Greek Acropolis, and the Roman pub, but the music we enjoy today would be nothing without the sustained and generally supportive history of the Christian church. Like everything else, musicians were affected by the slings and arrows of outrageous reformation, but they got off lightly. The English composer John Marbeck (1505–85) came to grief in 1543 when, with three others, he was arrested and imprisoned in London for allegedly criticizing the Mass that King Henry VIII still knew and loved. (It is often forgotten that as far as he was concerned, Henry VIII died a Roman Catholic, in 1547.) The four heretics were sentenced to be burned at the stake, but at the final hour Marbeck gained a reprieve, some say because the king liked his music, others that it was widely held that Marbeck was a simple musician and could not have authored the heresy of which he was accused. The others were burned at Windsor. While it may only be partly true, it is nice to think that Marbeck got a royal pardon because he was a musician, even if that means that he was considered to have been dim-witted!

This sorry episode is of course exceptional, and even though Tallis, Philips, and others had to mind their step during the Protestant and Counter Reformations in Europe, we have inherited a wonderful treasure store of music that, in our more enlightened and ecumenical times, transcends its historical contexts to become fine and beautiful vehicles for spirituality and praise.

Given this heritage and the history of Western music, it is hardly surprising that churches still tend to make music to the glory of God. The social, unifying, and cultural benefits of a musical life are almost sufficient in themselves, but with the added dimension of a spiritual mandate, music-making becomes necessary. How could we worship without song? How would we manage without our choir? Historically the church was always the greatest patron of music and other arts, and it is easy to forget, now that we have vast CD libraries and centuries' worth of manuscripts, that much music was composed for the church, often for a specific occasion. Court composers were appointed to write music for worship, the most famous being Bach, who wrote a cantata for each Sunday of the church year, usually during the preceding week. The universe would be the poorer if he had not composed the *St. Matthew* and *St. John Passions.* The teamwork and skill required to put on those works is notable, for there cannot have been much rehearsal time and mutual attentiveness was paramount.

Music as Ministry

While the church has employed composers, Bach, Mozart, and Bruckner among them, it is only recently that church musicians have been seen as having anything approaching a ministerial role. Yet it follows from what we have seen that to have a church musician as anything less is to miss an opportunity and to fail to employ their full talents as leader and artistic theologian. Not all theology is verbal, nor is all worship, and so to neglect music or musicians is to miss something. We might be reminded here of the Benedictine idea of work as prayer: a monk working in the garden or peeling the potatoes can make that task part of daily prayer, not only offering it to God, but praying to God through that activity. Making music is little different: it is an activity through which God can be praised, and is a piece of work that can itself be prayerful. On the other hand, we might also want to wonder, how much more prayerful can making music be than peeling potatoes!

Indeed, good liturgy and good ecclesiastical performance often seek to be unnoticed: nothing in liturgy should be self-conscious or attention-seeking in itself. The requirement of all involved in leadership of this kind is not to be noticed, but to direct attention to the divine dimensions of worship and praise. Music and liturgy point us to the worship of God, not to the priest, servers, or organist themselves.

Many church musicians are rightly affirmed for their skills and what we may even consider their divine gift. Thus it is to all church musicians, to music lovers who know and love Christ, and to those whose spiritual gift it is to partake from the pews, that I offer my reflections on this collection of anthems and other church music, sung so beautifully by Gloriæ Dei Cantores.

The choir Gloriæ Dei Cantores (www.gdcchoir.org), the home choir of the Community of Jesus, led by Elizabeth Patterson, contributed significantly to the inspiration for this book. The life calling on the members of this choir to the spiritual and artistic authenticity of their craft, and their love for it and for each other, is made manifest through their singing. This accompanying compilation CD bears witness to their name, which means "Singers to the Glory of God," and to their mission: to illuminate truth and beauty through choral artistry and to glorify God through a faithful interpretation of two millennia of sacred choral music.

May the music that unites us bless us and direct our hearts heavenward, in sound and in silence.

30 REFLECTIONS
WITH MUSIC

1. Viadana • *Exsultate, justi*
CD Track 1—2:15

Exsultate, justi, in Domino; rectos decet collaudatio. Confitemini Domino in cithara; in psalterio decem chordarum psallite illi. Cantate ei canticum novum; bene psallite ei in vociferatione. Exsultate, justi, in Domino; rectos decet collaudatio.

Rejoice in the LORD, O you righteous. Praise befits the upright. Praise the LORD with the lyre; make melody to him with the harp of ten strings. Sing to him a new song; play skillfully on the strings, with loud shouts. Rejoice in the LORD, O righteous. Praise befits the upright.

Text: Psalm 33:1–3
Music: Lodovico Grossi da Viadana (c. 1560–1627)

We begin, appropriately, with a psalm about praising God with instruments and voices. While this psalm resonates with the various ways we worship musically today, it also gives us an insight into the ways in which temple worship took place many years before the birth of Christ. The lyre is like a handheld harp, sometimes with ten strings, that was used to accompany singing. The psalmist believes that the ability of the player is important, for when the instrument is played skillfully, the Lord is pleased. Some people today feel that it does not matter how well liturgical music is played, but that it is more important that everyone joins in. Others prefer to take the view that any offering of praise should be as excellent as possible, and that highly skilled musicians should lead and perform music in church, whether the style be ancient or modern. A psalmist's injunction to be skillful is as relevant today as it was then. We assume that the music of heaven is better than any we can produce on earth, so that while we strive for excellence, we may occasionally feel that we are transported to heaven on a wave of wondrous music sung beautifully. However, we never reach perfection musically any more than we do morally or spiritually. Yet in all these spheres we strive to do well and please God, knowing we fall short, but also aware that our prayers are heard and our sins forgiven.

Alongside excellence, the psalmist extols the virtue of novelty in music. It is almost as if he is suggesting that God gets bored with the same old music and relishes a "new song." We hear this several times in the Psalms. "He put a new song in my mouth, a song of praise to our God" (Psalm 40:3a) reveals that the new song that God desires is also given to us by him. For the ability to worship God in word and song is itself a gift of God. Psalm 144:9 echoes this psalm identically: "I will sing a new song to you, O God; upon a ten-stringed harp I will play to you," and Psalm 98 begins with the same injunction: "O sing to the LORD a new song, for he has done marvelous things" (v. 1a). We find the same divine desire for new music at the end of the Bible, when in the book of Revelation we hear of singing before the opening of the scrolls (Revelation 5:9) and then as the redeemed take their place in the new heaven: "They sing a new song before the throne and before the four living creatures and before the elders. No one could learn that song except the one hundred forty-four thousand who have been redeemed from the earth" (Revelation 14:3). The message is fairly clear, there is new music in heaven, and we should be cautious when confining ourselves to old hymns! By the same token, budding composers, especially in the church, should feel encouraged.

On the other hand, there is already much beautiful music around us on earth, and one of the privileges of living in the twenty-first century is the widespread availability of a wide range of music. With iPods and other MP3 players, car stereos, and airline music feeds, we can have music wherever we go now, and it is ironic that many people spend so much of their lives "plugged in" to music that the prospect of live, prayerful praise is strange to them. One can spend so much time surrounded by music that it ceases to be valued or even noticed, but becomes simply part of the background of modern life. This is perhaps why God likes "new music," for new music often grabs our attention and makes us focus on what we are doing. Some hymns, for example, are so well known that we can sing them without really trying, and the words pass us by on a wave of familiarity. Our worship needs to be kept alive, kept moving by the familiar but also awakened by that which is new, challenging, or striking. Newness in music is not therefore necessarily something freshly composed, but something newly encountered. That is where the great treasure house of renaissance, classical, and Victorian music can be a great boon, arousing our hearts and souls with a new experience of that which is old and unfamiliar. Fame and greatness do not always go hand in hand, and for both singers and listeners there is much to discover in the anthems of the church.

One composer whose music is not so well known, but who is worth getting to know, is Viadana, who lived and worked in Mantua, Padua, Rome, and Cremona between 1594 and 1608. Thereafter, he was based in Venice and then Fano. He had been born in Viadana (hence his name), which is near Parma and he spent much of his life as a monk of the order of Minor Observants. We begin our musical pilgrimage with his setting of the opening verses of Psalm 33. It is an airy, almost dancelike piece, rhythmical yet graceful, that both begins and ends with the opening verse of the psalm: "Rejoice in the Lord. O you righteous. Praise befits the upright." We can hardly begin with better encouragement than that!

Lord, give us grace to find new ways to sing your praise and to discover your hand in both ancient and modern music, for in Christ you are the same yesterday, today, and for ever. Amen.

2. Rubbra • *Nunc Dimittis in A-flat*
CD Track 2—2:11

Lord, now lettest thou thy servant depart in peace:
according to thy word.
For mine eyes have seen: thy salvation,
Which thou hast prepared: before the face of all people;
To be a light to lighten the Gentiles: and to be the glory of
thy people Israel.
Glory be to the Father, and to the Son, and to the Holy Ghost;
As it was in the beginning, is now, and ever shall be: world
without end. Amen.

Text: The Book of Common Prayer, 1662 (Luke 2:30–32)
Music: Edmund Rubbra (1901–86)

The two canticles called the *Magnificat* and the *Nunc Dimittis* are essential ingredients in the service of Evensong, which forms the staple of the spiritual diet of the English Cathedral and College Choir tradition. The *Magnificat* is the song of acceptance by the Virgin Mary and is sung in response to the annunciation of the angel Gabriel (see Luke 1:46–55) and is sung or said after the first reading from Scripture. The second reading follows the *Magnificat* and then comes the briefer and more poignant *Nunc Dimittis*. Literally, the title means "Now dismiss," and as with the *Magnificat*, the title is derived from the first words of the Latin version. Neither canticle was originally spoken or written in Latin, but arrived in the Prayer Book of 1662 from the earlier Roman Catholic offices of vespers and compline.

The biblical origin of the canticles is significant. They are not hymns, but are more akin to psalms, being utterly biblical in origin and nature. The *Nunc Dimittis* is uttered by Simeon, a righteous and devout man who was "looking forward to the consolation of Israel, and the Holy Spirit rested on him. It had been revealed to him by the Holy Spirit that he would not see death before he had seen the Lord's Messiah. Guided by the Spirit, Simeon came into the temple; and when the parents brought in the child Jesus, to do for him what was customary under the law, Simeon took him in his arms and praised God" (Luke 2:25–28). The meaning is clear in the passage: this old and faithful man is seeing the salvation on which he has built his faith. His encounter with the baby Christ is a reward, a revelation, a blessing beyond compare. It is so beautiful, so meaningful, and so inspiring that we can remind ourselves of it every evening (although how often do we remember its context even when saying or singing the *Nunc Dimittis?*).

The *Nunc Dimittis* is found in the daily office not to help us remember Simeon as such, but to help us focus on the fact that he saw the real thing: the Christ of God, incarnate, and he held him in his own old arms. Mary and Joseph must have felt a little nervous, handing over their forty-day-old baby to a frail, elderly man, but they were no doubt persuaded and encouraged by the gleam in his eye and the strength of his faith. A little baby does indeed bring much joy, and many count it a privilege to be able to embrace the hope of the future in this way. We are all Simeons when we hold a baby, and there is something basically human, yet also profoundly divine, when the old welcome and embrace the young like this. Such gestures speak of continuity, hope, and delight and mirror the created order.

These same elements—continuity, hope, delight, and order—are the lynchpins of daily office prayer, and this is perhaps why the *Nunc Dimittis* is so beloved and seems so right for the end of the day. In addition to Evensong, however, it is also appropriate for funerals. In many churches there is still a strong tradition of reciting or singing it while carrying the deceased down the aisle of the church for the last time. The rich English of "Lord, now lettest thou thy servant depart in peace" resonates with that mysterious blend of finality and hope with which a funeral is imbued. Old Simeon's prayer expresses the great hope of salvation, communion with God, and a restful peace in God's presence, but it never lets us pretend that earthly life is not over. Yet as the coffin is carried out, the Gloria is said or sung: praise of God for the door opening to eternal life. Often with a church funeral, the deceased pilgrim has been a regular worshiper, and this is their final journey, out from the church, into the graveyard or hearse, and into eternity. Many would agree that there are no better words than the *Nunc Dimittis* to serve this occasion and purpose.

The setting of the *Nunc Dimittis* with its partner the *Magnificat* by Edmund Rubbra was written in 1949, the year after he converted to Roman Catholicism. Nevertheless, it falls very much within the English church music tradition in which Rubbra received his musical education: he studied at Reading University and London's Royal College of Music with Gustav Holst (1874–1934). Sometimes Holst was unavailable for lessons, so Rubbra had to settle for Ralph Vaughan Williams (1872–1958) instead! With such a pedigree (despite having a poor background in the Midlands town of Northampton), Rubbra had a significant career as a composer, teacher, and critic, ending his days in the Chiltern hills, thirty miles northwest of London. In addition to choral music, he wrote eleven symphonies, separate concerti for violin, viola, and piano, and also a "Fanfare for Europe," specially commissioned to mark the UK's entry into the European Economic Community in 1972. Scored for six trumpets, it is based on the notes E-E-C!

Rubbra's cathedral music is not easy, but it is rewarding both to sing and to hear. His setting of the *Nunc Dimittis* may sound modern, but is also tranquil. Just as the old man, Simeon, gently welcomed the Christ child into a world in need of salvation, so we too can embrace the words of the *Nunc Dimittis* in such a way that our earthly songs of hope may echo the praise and glory of our Savior that reverberates into eternity.

Lord, for now, let us welcome your salvation, and see the reality of your presence with our own eyes; and when our time of departure comes, may we see you face to face and dwell in the midst of your glory for ever. Amen.

3. Hylton Stewart • *Psalm 137* (Chant)
CD Track 3—3:08

By the waters of Babylon we sat down and wept: when we
remembered thee, O Sion.

As for our harps, we hanged them up: upon the trees that
are therein.

For they that led us away captive required of us then a song, and
melody in our heaviness: Sing us one of the songs of Sion.

How shall we sing the Lord's song: in a strange land?

If I forget thee, O Jerusalem: let my right hand forget her
cunning.

If I do not remember thee, let my tongue cleave to the roof of my
mouth: yea, if I prefer not Jerusalem above my chief joy.

Remember the children of Edom, O Lord, in the day of
Jerusalem: how they said, Down with it, down with it,
even to the ground.

O daughter of Babylon, wasted with misery: yea, happy
shall he be that rewardeth thee, as thou hast served us.

Blessed shall he be that taketh thy children: and throweth
them against the stones.

Glory be to the Father, and to the Son, and to the Holy Ghost;

As it was in the beginning, is now, and ever shall be: world
without end. Amen.

Text: *Psalm 137* (The Book of Common Prayer 1662)
Music: Charles Hylton Stewart (1884–1932)

Most of the services of Morning and Evening Prayer are made
up of sacred poetry, hymns, canticles, and the ancient psalms.
The Psalter is sometimes referred to as the "Hymnbook of the
First Temple," a description that reminds us of the great age of the
Psalms. They have great poetic, prayerful, and portable value. The
experiences they relate are fundamentally human, and the emotions,

desires, and frustrations of the psalmist (whether David or not) are ones to which we can often relate at various times in our lives. For while we can "read" them with the eyes of a Christian, they were written at a time when knowledge of Christ was a mere hope. As such they provide us with insight into a more earthy, almost primitive understanding of the relationship between the human and the divine. Christ is our mediator in prayer (Hebrews 7:23–27), but the early singers of psalms had no such intermediary, the prayer and the praise were addressed directly to God in bold, or even brazen ways.

This is not to say that psalms are un-Christian texts. Some can be seen as referring to Christ (Psalm 23); or representing the voice of the church (Psalm 126); or may even be seen as words of Christ, such as Psalm 22, words from which ("My God, my God, why have you forsaken me?") are central to the crucifixion narrative. Other psalms, however, present difficulties for Christians, in that they express sentiments or desires that many would argue are un-Christian. Psalm 58 is not very edifying when it says: "O God, break the teeth in their mouths; tear out the fangs of the young lions, O LORD! Let them vanish like water that runs away; like grass let them be trodden down and wither. Let them be like the snail that dissolves into slime; like the untimely birth that never sees the sun" (Psalm 58:6–8). The next psalm has its moments too: "Rouse yourself, come to my help and see! You, LORD God of hosts, are God of Israel. Awake to punish all the nations; spare none of those who treacherously plot evil. . . . For the cursing and lies that they utter, consume them in wrath; consume them until they are no more. Then it will be known to the ends of the earth that God rules over Jacob" (Psalm 59:4b–6, 12–13). Unpleasant as the poetry may be, it expresses human vindictiveness, and none of us are immune to that.

Some of the most unkind verses in the Psalms come at the end of Psalm 137, and when sung in churches, the final two verses are often expunged. When Charles Hylton Stewart was writing chants and organ music for English Cathedral choirs, the convention of omitting Psalm 58 and the end of Psalm 137 was well established. He was organist of Rochester Cathedral in Kent from 1916 until 1930, in spite of the fact that he also became organist of Chester Cathedral (in the Northwest of England) in 1920. In September 1932, he was appointed organist of the king's private chapel at Windsor Castle, but died in November of the same year. This chant, used for Psalm 137, is an emotionally charged one, more suited to the opening theme of lament, rather than of vengeance and malice to which the psalm ultimately turns. Often sung without organ accompaniment to create an austere, uncluttered, peaceful atmosphere, the chant alternates between unison and harmony, aiding clarity of diction and narrowing our attention onto the words sung.

The psalm itself is a lament, sung by the Israelites who have become Hebrew slaves in Babylon. In 597 BC, King Nebuchadnezzar (also known as Nebuchadrezzar II) invaded Jerusalem and installed Zedekiah as king. Within ten years Zedekiah rebelled, provoking a second attack, the destruction of the temple, and the exile of many Jews to Babylon. Psalm 137 relates a firsthand experience of this exile, and we recognize something sadly all too familiar today. In recent years we have witnessed terrible tragedies of dispossession and exile among the peoples of the Balkans, Middle East, Rwanda, Sudan, and Eritrea. As in pre-Christian times, war, violence, religious division, and struggle for land and resources all play their part in the drama of exile. We may have no need to sing this psalm as we worship in comfortable churches today, but even in the peace of choral Evensong, we sing it in order to remember the plight of the dispossessed, to empathize with every dimension of the emotions they felt then and now, and to pray for the alleviation of injustice and violence in all the Babylons of our modern age.

Father, have mercy on those who are displaced, terrorized, or alienated. Grant to all leaders a spirit of justice and reconciliation that they may pursue what is good and right for the nations of the earth, and give each one of us the perseverance to pray and act for a better world. Amen.

4. Rachmaninov • *Bogoroditse Devo*
(*Ave Maria* from Vespers)
CD Track 4—2:43

Bogoroditse Devo, raduissya, Blagodatnaya, Mariye,
Gospod s Toboyu.
Blagoslovyena Ti v zhenah, i blagosloven plod chreva
Tvoyego, yako Spassa rodila, yesi dush nashih.

Rejoice O Virgin Mother of God. Mary, full of grace, the
   Lord is with you.
Blessed are you among women, and blessed is the fruit of
   your womb: for you have borne the savior of our souls.

Text: From the Liturgy of Vespers, based on Luke 1:41–45
Music: Sergei Rachmaninov (1873–1943)

Now we turn to a world of musical prayer that sounds culturally and linguistically different from choral Evensong, but is not so far removed from it. Vespers was, to some extent, subsumed into the Anglican service of Evensong, where it was combined with elements from compline (the night office). But vespers has remained intact in both Roman Catholic and Eastern Orthodox communities. No setting of vespers is more famous that that by Sergei Rachmaninov. Many associate Rachmaninov with his popular and exquisite piano concerti, and perhaps his symphonies. Others know his opera *Aleko*, or the lovely *Symphonic Dances*, or tone poem *The Isle of the Dead*. All are worth exploring, with their rich romanticism, sweeping melodies, and luscious harmonies. So it is no surprise that Rachmaninov's setting of the vespers is equally attractive, but in a way that carries us deep into the beauty of our own souls, transporting us to other realms of music and prayer.

First performed in Moscow on March 10, 1915, and dedicated to a notable authority on Russian church music, Stepan Vasilievich Smolensky, Rachmaninov's so-called "Vespers" also includes matins, for it was customary to elide the two services for an all-night Saturday vigil. There is no accompaniment for the voices, as Orthodox tradition forbids the use of instruments in church. Smolensky was the director of the Moscow Synodal School (and their choir) and lectured at the Moscow Conservatory where Rachmaninov was a student between 1890–91. In this period, a blend of Russian nationalism and a desire to reintegrate Russian folk songs and old liturgical music into a religious musical tradition that had basically become Westernized created a revival of interest in Russian liturgy. Rachmaninov's first setting was a Eucharist setting of the Liturgy of St. John Chrysostom, composed in 1910.

Like much Orthodox Church choral music, the texts of these works are in Old Church Slavonic, the ancient liturgical language of the Eastern Orthodox Church. It was originally spoken by southern Slavic tribes who invaded the Balkan Peninsula in the sixth and seventh centuries, settling as Bulgarians, Serbs, and others; hence Old Church Slavonic is sometimes called Old Bulgarian. Brothers Cyril and Methodius (who share a feast day with St. Valentine, February 14) invented the Cyrillic and Glagolitic alphabets respectively, when working as missionaries in South Slavic lands, in order to translate the Bible into a written form. While ordinary people did not speak Church Slavonic as such, literature and liturgy employed it. It was an official written language in Czech, Moravian, Bulgarian, Serbian, Russian, and Lithuanian lands for a long time, ultimately being replaced by Latin or by national languages such as Russian. Nevertheless, Old Church Slavonic is still the official language of the Russian Orthodox Church, and hence we encounter it here.

Vespers itself begins with an invocation to worship, during which the veil behind the Holy Doors of the iconostasis (icon screen) is pulled aside and the doors opened. Preceded by a deacon with a lighted candle, the priest enters and gives an initial blessing. Then an abbreviated form of Psalm 103 is sung ("Bless the Lord my soul") during which incense is wafted, on the altar, the icons, and the people. Psalm 1 is sung ("Blessed is the man") with alleluias. Contrary to the Orthodox tradition of standing during liturgies, the people sit for this part of the service. The ancient Greek hymn *Phos hilarion* ("Hail gladdening light") follows, and lamps are gradually lit. Then the priest and deacon enter the Holy of Holies, passing through the Holy Doors that are already open. This is the climax of the service and the *Nunc Dimittis* is sung. Then follows the *Ave Maria*: *Bogoroditse Devo* is the final, gently joyful part of vespers, and is followed by a priestly blessing, while the lights are dimmed and the doors closed before the vigil of matins begins. Thus, although this piece concludes vespers, it appears barely a third of the way through the complete vigil setting that Rachmaninov composed.

There is little evidence that Rachmaninov had much time for the Orthodox Church, but he was fascinated by its music, and after the two liturgies he set in 1910 and 1915 were highly acclaimed in secular and sacred circles, he seemed prepared to compose more. However, the Revolution of 1917 put an end to any further liturgical work: religion was banned and Rachmaninov fled to the United States. Yet we should also be aware that the All-night Vigil was hardly intended for liturgical use: it makes more sense and was undoubtedly intended as an hour-long concert work.

Since the vigil music is inherently prayerful, containing ancient prayers of the church, such as the *Phos hilarion* and *Ave Maria*, we need not worry too much about Rachmaninov's intentions for his enthralling choral music. In our age of recorded music and choral excellence, we find our prayers can be blessed by a musical dimension. We can have daily prayer and daily music. Perhaps like me, you might consider a day without music to be a day lacking something pleasant, rewarding, edifying, or even vital.

Prayer takes many forms, at many times and in different places, but in our age, there is potential for praying through the beauties of a recording. Whether in concert performance, or on CD, any rendition of a work that has its textual roots in Elizabeth's greeting of her cousin Mary, newly called to be the Mother of the Son of God, and is translated into an ancient language, and set to music so prayerfully, may allow us to briefly ascend to the music of heaven.

O Lord, fill our souls with the joy of your salvation, that day or night, the music of our prayer may rise to you like incense. Amen.

5. Kedrov • *Otche nash (Our Father)*
CD Track 5—3:18

*Otche nash, ije yesi na nebeseh, da svyatitsya imya Tvoye,
da priidyet tsarstvie Tvoye, da budyet volya Tvoya yako
na nebesi i na zyemgli. Chlyeb nash nasushnyi dashd nam
dnyes i astavi nam dolghi nasha, yakoje i myi astavlyayem
doljnikam na shim, i nye vedi nas va iskusheniye, no izbavi
nas ot luka vago.*

Our Father, who art in heaven, hallowed be thy name;
thy kingdom come; thy will be done; on earth as it is in
heaven. Give us this day our daily bread. And forgive us our
trespasses, as we forgive those who trespass against us. And
lead us not into temptation; but deliver us from evil.

Text: The Lord's Prayer (Luke 11:1–4)
Music: Nikolai Kedrov, Sr. (1871–1940)

Very little is known about Nikolai Kedrov, the composer of this
famous and popular setting of the Lord's Prayer. Born in Russia,
like Rachmaninov he emigrated to the United States. His son, also
called Nikolai (1905–81), was a composer as well. His anthem consists
not only of the Lord's Prayer, but also the invocation to pray, uttered
by the priest. Such invocations are familiar to us: "As our Savior has
taught us, so we pray" serves a similar purpose in gathering everyone
to speak or sing together. Indeed, Kedrov's setting of the Lord's Prayer
has become so popular in the Orthodox Church that the congregation
may join in, and so a priestly introduction is helpful.

The music is not complex. It begins with a C major chord
repeated ten times, then the melody line moves up a semitone (all-
male chorus versions are transposed into other keys). This gradual,
subtle movement sets the tone of the piece: there are to be no
surprises, no sudden jolts, but rather a steady, measured buildup,

not of tension, but of profound and passionate prayer. There is a key climax on the words "and forgive us our trespasses," which then recedes as a gentle cascade back to a restful end. The overall sound world is archetypically Eastern Orthodox, created by close harmony, and a pace that admits no pressure from any external force to speed up or slow down for any reason other than devotion. This is music to bathe in, to join in with, to pray through and with. Yet there is passion too: Church Slavonic uses the vocative case, which means that there is a greater sense of imploring than in English versions, so here it is more like: "O Our Father."

There is no "Amen" at the end of the piece, because it is not the end of the piece. Just as the priest intones an invocation to pray, he continues afterward, with the words, "For thine is the kingdom, and the power, and the glory: of the Father, and of the Son, and of the Holy Spirit, now and ever, and unto the ages of ages." and only then do the people sing "Amen." The Lord's Prayer is very much part of the liturgy with the priest and people in dialogue, the priest both leading and joining with them in prayer. The word *liturgy*, derived from Greek, means "work of the people," and in Orthodox Eucharistic liturgies, there is a real sense that the singing of the Lord's Prayer, the church family prayer, is a common work of devotion. A Christian knows the Lord's Prayer, and uses it.

The Lord's Prayer derives from an account of the occasion when the disciples ask Jesus how to pray (Luke 11:1–4). Yet the Lord's Prayer also embodies a microcosm of faith. It begins with our relationship with God who is "our Father." He is like a parent and he is ours. In faith we share so much as the body of Christ. Yet there is also an "otherness" of God: he is both mysterious and holy (hallowed): he is better, bigger, wiser, and purer than we can ever be. The Lord's Prayer also affirms God's supremacy: it is God's kingdom that shall come and God's will that shall be done. We bow to no other and strive to live according to his ordinances.

The Lord's Prayer connects earth and heaven, that place of God, of hope, prepared for us by Christ. Heaven is not a distant or imaginary place, but as real as salvation and divinity itself. In the Lord's Prayer, we bring a little heaven upon ourselves as we implore God to rule earth as heaven.

The Lord's Prayer expresses our basic needs for food and forgiveness. Physical food and spiritual forgiveness, without which we cannot be saved: the Lord provides both to those who turn to him in faith. Yet, forgiveness must be administered as well as received. We do as we would be done by: we cannot expect to have our needs met when we neglect or refuse to meet others' needs.

Temptation comes next, and there is plenty of that available. Our only defense against temptation is divine. We pray that God would lead us away from that which can harm us, or deprive us of our faith. Sadly so many are led into the temptation to believe that faith, God, and Christ are irrelevant. Any reading of the Lord's Prayer reveals that that cannot be so, for the Lord's Prayer also emphasizes the reality of evil. We beseech God to deliver us, but we hardly need prayer to remind us that evil is very much around us.

At the heart of the Lord's Prayer is the request for daily bread, implying daily prayer. The Lord's Prayer reminds us that our faith is not only enacted in church, or only weekly. Our faith is daily, even hourly. Faith is a constant, sustaining us in good or ill, sorrow or joy. It serves us and sustains us in every place and situation, not just in church. Faith is supremely expressed, articulated, and taught in the Lord's Prayer, which Jesus himself gave us. As Christians, let us know it, and use it!

Lord, we need food and forgiveness. By your grace, let us never take your blessings for granted, but live and pray as witnesses to the peace you bring to us and the loving kindness with which you surround us day by day. Amen.

6. Gregorian Chant • *Psalm 150*

CD Track 6—1:27

Laudate Dominum in sanctis Ejus.
Laudate Erum firmamentis virtutis Ejus.
Laudate Dominum. Laudate Eum in virtutibus Ejus.
Laudate Eum secundum multitudinem magnitudinis Ejus.
Laudate Eum in sono tubae.
Laudate Eum. Laudate Dominum.
Laudate Eum. Laudate Eum in timpano et choro,
Laudate Eum in cordis et organo;
Laudate Eum in cymbalis bene jubilantionibus.
Laudate Eum, omnis spiritus laudate Dominum.

Praise the LORD! Praise God in his sanctuary;
praise him in his mighty firmament!
Praise him for his mighty deeds;
praise him according to his surpassing greatness!
Praise him with trumpet sound;
praise him with lute and harp!
Praise him with tambourine and dance;
praise him with strings and pipe!
Praise him with clanging cymbals;
praise him with loud clashing cymbals!
Let everything that breathes praise the LORD!
Praise the LORD!

Text: Psalm 150
Music: Gregorian Chant Mode II

Gregorian chant was the musical staple of the church between
the fourth and fourteenth centuries, and has also been known
in different places and times as "plainsong" or "plainchant." *Plain*

is to be contrasted with florid or fancy. Fancy music was frowned upon by the medieval church, because, as the Council of Tours declared in 813, "Everything that can lead the ears and the eyes astray and can corrupt the vigor of the mind is to be away from God's priests, for it is by tickling the ear and beguiling the eye that the multitude of sins generally enters the soul." Chant is the foundation of almost all the music we have today. Its roots are to be found along with the beginnings of all Christian worship, in synagogues and temples. Early Christian liturgy was hardly different from its Jewish counterpart, and the use of the psalms is still common to Christianity and Judaism. Psalm singing and chant were married together in antiquity, and the relationship is still very much alive.

In the fourth century, Bishop Ambrose of Milan decreed that four scales, or modes, could be used for liturgical singing. In the sixth century, Pope Gregory supervised extensive liturgical revision, adding four more modes to the repertoire and as a consequence Gregorian chant is named after him. Around the same time (597), he sent Augustine to England to convert King Ethelbert, and the monks who met the king at Thanet sang Gregorian chant when they landed. After the Norman invasion of 1066, the French attempted to introduce their manner of singing into England's churches, but the abbot of Glastonbury would have none of it, and had archers on duty in the upper part of the abbey, who shot at the French monks if they sang in the "foreign style."

In modern music we only use two of the eight modes that Gregory authorized, and these we call major and minor. A mode is not quite like a key—it is a type of scale. A mode is defined, not by the *notes* it employs, as C major is defined by C-D-E-F-G-A-B-C, but rather by the *intervals* between the notes. The C major scale is the Ionian mode. Modes were named after Greek cultures whose musical system they were supposed to emulate, but this was not founded upon any factual evidence. The mode used for Psalm 150 here is mode II, known as *plagalis protus* and based upon the apparently ancient Hypodorian mode.

Scripture was set in a manner like a spoken style. By the eleventh century, chants were being used in all services, especially in the Eucharist. Also in the eleventh century, notation (written music) began to appear. Guido of Arezzo (995–1050) first had the idea of placing the notes on parallel lines. He invented a four-line system, not the five that most music employs today. Once notation had developed, it became possible to write more than one musical part at a time, and so harmony and counterpoint were born. Nevertheless, Gregorian chant remained in use in its original form and is still very much with us today.

As Gregorian chant is simple in structure, it is appropriate for prayer and spiritual contemplation. Sometimes our worship and prayer is very elaborate, but it can be helpful to reflect upon the simple facts of our faith. Just as we may empty ourselves in quiet prayer, we may empty our music, returning to our spiritual roots in an attempt to unclutter ourselves when we come into God's presence. Thus, many people who enjoy meditation and quiet prayer find plainsong conducive. Usually sung responsorially, the first line of a psalm verse may be intoned by a cantor, with the congregation responding, or, in places where plainsong is the usual mode of prayer, such as in monasteries, or at the Community of Jesus on Cape Cod, the congregation is effectively divided down the length of the chancel or church, with the sides responding to one another. In European cathedrals, the two sides were called *Cantores* (the cantor's side) and *Decani* (the dean's side) and these names (or simply *Dec* and *Can*) are still used today where choirs are divided. Between them the praise of God is bounced from side to side, like a ball of prayer kept aloft in a joyous but contemplative dialogue that is both reflective and attentive.

Gregorian chant is particularly fitting for this last psalm, in which God is specifically extolled. Everything that has breath can praise the Lord, and plainsong is a particularly disciplined but expressive form of exhaling musical prayer. Psalm 150 is often set to music, for obvious reasons: at one end of the scale we have humble plainsong, while composers such as Stravinsky and Bruckner have composed large-scale, complex settings that truly do allow the trumpet to sound!

The long history of chanting gives us a link with our Christian origins, for we can sing the same music that our spiritual ancestors sang. Doing so can make us aware that while our worship is located today, our prayers ascend to heaven with those of all Christians in every age. While Christ is the same yesterday and today (Hebrews 13:8), we are always finding new dimensions in worship, especially where music is concerned. Gregorian chant can be a spiritual discovery, because for some it can be both very old and brand new.

Lord, we worship you with hearts and hands and voices, in the breath of song, the plucking of strings and the blowing of brass. As all creation worships you in song and silence, so we employ every instrument to your praise, for you are God; Father, Son, and Holy Spirit, now and for ever. Amen.

7. Ives • *Psalm 100*

CD Track 7—2:05

"Make a joyful noise unto the LORD, all ye lands.
Serve the LORD with gladness: come before his presence
with singing.
Know ye that the LORD he is God: it is he that hath made
us, and not we ourselves; we are his people, and the sheep
of his pasture.
Enter into his gates with thanksgiving, and into his courts
with praise: be thankful unto him, and bless his name.
For the LORD is good; his mercy is everlasting; and his truth
endureth to all generations." (KJV)

Text: Psalm 100 (*Jubilate*)
Music: Charles Ives (1874–1954)

This psalm is often referred to simply by its Latin title, which is the first word: *jubilate*. This word hardly needs translating, as from it we derive celebratory words such as *jubilation* and *jubilee*. Psalm 100 is a celebration of joy, an exclamation of jubilant praise for our God who creates us, sustains us, and forgives us. These are the three key themes of this psalm, which is frequently sung in liturgical worship. The English Book of Common Prayer of 1662 recommends it as an alternative to the *Benedictus* sung or said every day at mattins (Morning Prayer). As such there are many settings of it; quite a few from the twentieth century. In England, both Benjamin Britten (1913–76) and William Walton (1902–83) wrote fine settings, while America's most illustrious version may be the one by Charles Ives.

The hundredth psalm is quite short, so musical settings are not lengthy, and since Ives does not include a doxology ("Glory be. . . .")

at the end, it is particularly brief. Ives's word setting is uncluttered
so the text comes through clearly, even in a brief central section
when the choir divides to sing different words, it is still possible
to discern the text. Ives made many settings of psalms, among
them Psalms 67, 24, 150; his most famous is Psalm 90. Having
been a salaried church organist in his hometown of Danbury,
Connecticut, from the age of fourteen, and later at Center
Church, Princeton, Ives was well-schooled in Protestant church
music, as well as in American vernacular music. He remained a
church organist until 1902, the year that he composed *Psalm 100*.
Having studied music at Yale, he followed his father's deathbed
advice and embarked upon a career as an insurance broker,
always keeping his prolific musical interests as a sideline.

In many respects, but especially musically, Ives was influenced
by his father, George. George Ives had been the youngest
bandleader in the Yankee army during the Civil War, and while
it was largely due to his father's efforts and encouragement that
Charles became so proficient so young, his father also taught him
respect for and delight in American folk music, hymnody, and the
songs of Stephen Foster (1826–64). Once father and son heard
a stonemason singing rather badly, and in a comment that the
young Charles always remembered, George said: "Look into his
face and hear the music of the ages. Don't pay too much attention
to the sounds, for if you do, you may miss the music. You won't
get a wild, heroic ride to heaven on pretty little sounds."

The spiritual power of music from camp meetings and
marching bands inspired Ives throughout his life, and manifested
itself in his symphonies and choral music (his Third Symphony is
subtitled *The Camp Meeting*). A great musical innovator, Ives's
creative genius produced remarkable works, such as *Central Park
in the Dark* and *The Unanswered Question*, both of which employ
groups playing at the same time, but in different keys and meters.
Consequently Ives's influence on later avant-garde composers such
as John Cage (1912–92) was immensely significant.

Toward the end of his life, Ives basically stopped composing, but would occasionally add something to a spiritually intense, mammoth work he called the *Universe Symphony*. He was attempting "to paint the creation, the mysterious beginnings of all things . . . the evolution of all life in nature, of humanity from the great roots of life to the spiritual eternities, from the great inknown to the great unknown." Intended to be performed outside, with orchestras and choirs in valleys and on hillsides, it is not surprising that Ives never completed his attempt to match in music the Father's Creation.

Yet we do have his brief *Psalm 100*, which sets the psalmist's more modest description of our relationship to our Creator. As the second verse puts it, "It is he that hath made us, and not we ourselves." In just a few words, we are reminded of how we came to be. We were not made by our parents, or by doctors, or by storks, but by God. It is so easy to forget that we are creatures, not creators. Like Ives, we may be able to create marvelous music and art, but we must never lose sight of the fact that we ourselves are made by God. If we have children, we are procreating—creating with God. We become involved in a creative process, and it is not just up to us if new life is produced.

All of this has implications for recent research involving the use of stem cells, cloning, and the creation of embryos that are part human and part animal. While some nations ban research that may lead to or involve cloning, others welcome and encourage it. There is a certain irony in the fact that the first cloned animal, Dolly, was a sheep. She was bred in Edinburgh and was born in 1996, but only lived until 2003. We, God's people, made a sheep for new technological pastures, and there is still a debate as to whether the experiment was a success. Perhaps we should remember, as we push back the boundaries of medical technology, that life is God's gift to us, that we are the sheep of *his* pasture, and that it is he that has made us, not we ourselves.

O God, our Creator, who gives us freedom and responsibility that we must exercise, bless all who, by your grace, create works of beauty, and of healing power. May we, and all your children, hear your voice of love in the midst of the noise of the world and the clamor of dilemma, so that all your creation may live and thrive to your glory and praise. For you reign, Father, Son, and Holy Spirit, now and always. Amen.

8. Langlais • *Kyrie* from *Messe Solennelle*
CD Track 8—4:05

Kyrie eleison
Christe eleison
Kyrie eleison

Lord, have mercy.
Christ, have mercy.
Lord, have mercy.

Text: Propers of the Mass—Kyrie
Music: Jean Langlais (1907–91) from *Messe Solennelle*

The Eucharist, or Lord's Supper, is the ultimate commemoration of Jesus' suffering and death for our sins, and is central to Christian devotion and theology. To musicians, the word *Mass* is often used not so much as a term to describe what happens at an altar, but a generic term to describe a set of word-settings by a single composer, intended to accompany and enhance a celebration of the Eucharist. Some settings of the Mass, such as those by Bach and Beethoven, were hardly intended to be used in a liturgical setting (they are far too lengthy), and are too expensive and complicated for use other than in concert halls. Other Mass settings were clearly intended for liturgical use.

This is true of this setting by Jean Langlais. Although he was blind, he was taught by Paul Dukas (of "Sorcerer's Apprentice" fame) and the great organist Tournemire. His first job was as organist of the Parisian church of St. Pierre-de-Montrouge. He also taught at the school for the blind where he himself had studied, where he taught composition and conducted the choir in the singing of Bach and Palestrina. In 1945, he became organist at the church of St. Clotilde in Paris, a position previously held by César Franck and his former teacher Tournemire. He became a celebrity, especially in the United States, where he gave over 300 recitals between 1952 and 1981. Many of his works were written for churches in America: the *Missa Orbis Factor* was for the National Shrine of the Immaculate Conception in Washington, DC, where 7,000 people attended the first performance in 1969.

The *Messe Solennelle* was his first major choral work and was written in 1951 for use at St. Clotilde. The *solennelle* of the title does not make it solemn in the way we often understand the word, but refers to the type of Mass or Eucharist at which it might be used. Technically speaking, a solemn Mass is one at which a deacon and subdeacon are present, and at which the choir sings the propers. The propers are the texts that regularly occur, the Kyrie, Gloria, Sanctus and Benedictus, Credo, and Agnus Dei. Communion services in many denominations preserve most of these propers today (although in Advent and Lent it is customary to omit the Gloria). In musical settings, which are often performed apart from any liturgical context, these propers are often treated more as movements are in a choral symphony.

Langlais's *Solemn Mass* is not a concert piece, however, and is still heard in great cathedrals and churches today. Conventionally it opens with that most penitential part of the Mass, the Kyrie eleison. The organ is heard first, boldly but gently ushering in the opening plea for mercy. The organ always accompanies the choir and gives support to the chant-inspired melodies that Langlais has composed. As *Kyrie eleison* gives way to *Christe eleison* and then back to *Kyrie eleison*, the organ punctuates, increasing the volume and intensity between them such that the whole movement is a gradual crescendo of power and passion, until choir and organ reach a final *rallentando* (slowing up). The Kyrie is solemn in both senses of the word, liturgically speaking, but also in the gravitas that the music conveys and instills in the Eucharistic celebration.

The text of the Kyrie is the only part of our Communion service that is in Greek. Much of the Eucharist was translated into Latin in the early medieval period, but the Kyrie was untouched. *Kyrie* means *Lord*, and *Christe* means *Christ*, the anointed one. It is the Greek version of the Hebrew word *Messiah*. This text has been in use since the fourth century, persisting in daily prayer services as well as in Holy Communion. We say "Lord, have mercy" so frequently that it can seem unremarkable and automatic, and seeking God's mercy in worship can become so common and instinctive that we barely notice that we are doing so. Similarly, we tend to sing hymns without thinking about what we are really singing to ourselves or to God or to each other.

Langlais, let us remember, was blind. The poignancy of this fact, when allied to the greatness of his musical and technical achievement as organist and composer, is humbling. In the face of handicap and prejudice, Langlais breaks into our complacent, ungrateful, and fortunate lives with a music that makes any plea for mercy very real indeed.

The Kyrie is all about seeking forgiveness, not only for ourselves, and for any individual sins we may feel we have knowingly or unknowingly committed, but also for the sins of the world, past and present, which, as we study history or read our newspapers, we very much lament. We make our petition assured of God's forgiveness already manifested in Christ, but as we prepare to remember his offering of himself, which we commemorate in the bread and wine, we need also to remind ourselves of the sins for which he died. This we do in God's presence as we prepare to welcome our Savior. The *Kyrie* of Langlais's *Messe Solennelle* reminds us of the magnitude of mercy that we seek, and receive, and as such, it wakes us from any sleepy, unthinking request for mercy that may so easily pass us by at a Communion service. For it is only by the mercy and grace of God that we approach the Holy Table, the crumbs from which we are barely fit to gather.

Lord, have mercy. Christ, have mercy. Have mercy on us as we amble through life, often oblivious of our own sins and the afflictions of others. Make us always thankful for your great mercy and generosity, and by your Holy Spirit, help us see our sinfulness, that we may daily be renewed by your saving grace. Amen.

9. Mathias • *Gloria* from *Missa Brevis*
CD Track 9—4:32

Glory be to God on high,
and in earth peace, good will toward men.
We praise thee, we bless thee,
we worship thee, we glorify thee,
we give thanks to thee for thy great glory,
O Lord God, heavenly King,
God the Father Almighty.

O Lord, the only-begotten Son, Jesu Christ;
O Lord God, Lamb of God, Son of the Father,
that takest away the sins of the world,
have mercy upon us.
Thou that takest away the sins of the world,
receive our prayer.
Thou that sittest at the right hand of God the Father,
have mercy upon us.

For thou only art holy;
thou only art the Lord;
thou only, O Christ with the Holy Ghost,
art most high in the glory of God the Father. Amen.

Text: Propers of the Mass—Gloria (The Book of Common Prayer 1662)
Music: William Mathias (1934–92) from *Missa Brevis*

N ow we turn to the Gloria in excelsis, which is used in Eucharistic services most of the year. The Gloria has been used since at least the fifth century, although the Book of Common Prayer of

1552 and of 1662 place it at the end of the service, where it is sung in gratitude for the gifts of salvation and communion. Nowadays it is more often found early in the service. It is also appropriate as an opening hymn of praise.

Traditionally, the Gloria is omitted during Advent and Lent, giving a more somber feeling to the liturgies in those periods and preparing for its resplendent return at Christmas and Easter celebrations. The textual content of the Gloria is a reminder of both, even when those feasts are long past or way ahead. The opening lines recall the words of the angels to the shepherds in Bethlehem: "Glory to God in the highest heaven, and on earth peace among those whom he favors!" (Luke 2:14). Angels are messengers of God, and in the Bible we often find them bearing good news (gospel). They bring the Good News about the Incarnation, leading to redemption and eternal hope, which the Gloria extols so poetically.

While the author of the rest of the text is unknown, the Gloria is rather like a psalm, a hymn of praise to God in Christ who reigns in glory, receives our prayers, and displays infinite mercy. As with the Psalms, there is a great outpouring of joy, glorification of God for what he has done for us, and an acknowledgment of the work of Christ, who, as Lamb of God has taken away our sins. God as Trinity is praised in the final lines, and it is clear that this is the post-Easter, ascended Christ who is referred to and worshiped.

Settings of the Gloria usually begin and end joyfully, with a quieter, penitential central section. The sentiment of the text suggests such a structure, and many composers have taken advantage of it to create a balanced work that adapts emotionally to the words. Boisterous opening praise and thanksgiving gives way to acknowledgment of sin in the presence of the merciful Lamb of God, who, although reigning in glory, receives our humble prayer. Then the final lines extol with exuberant praise the holiness and Trinitarian unity of the Godhead.

An organ fanfare opens Mathias's brief setting, before the chorus enters with a jaunty tune. Repeated utterances of "we bless thee" and "we worship thee" emphasize joyful praise. The busy writing and repetition reminds us that *we* are involved in corporate, not individual praise. As we might expect, Mathias quiets down in mysterious recognition of the Lamb of God, and a blend of humble adoration with a note of fear and trembling can be detected in the writing. The music pauses before a reiteration of the trumpet fanfare and the third section, which carries the musical material of the first third into new realms, raising the spiritual and harmonic temperature to a final and jubilant *Amen*.

This *Missa Brevis* (Short Mass) typifies William Mathias's style and his attitude toward music. For him all music was celebratory, and he found it particularly appropriate to express it chorally. Many will have heard his specially commissioned anthem *Let All the People Praise Thee*, a joyous setting of words from Psalm 67 composed for the wedding of the Prince and Princess of Wales in 1981. His *Missa Brevis* was written for the Parish Church of St. Matthew's, Northampton, and was premiered in 1973 with Stephen Cleobury holding the baton. St. Matthew's has an illustrious cultural history, particularly during the period 1937–55 when Walter Hussey (1909–85) was vicar (as his father had been before him). Hussey was a true patron of the arts, commissioning for Northampton *Rejoice in the Lamb* by Benjamin Britten (1913–76), *Madonna and Child* by the English sculptor Henry Moore (1898–1986), a *Litany and Anthem for St. Matthew's Day* from W.H. Auden in 1945, and Graham Sutherland's *Crucifixion* painting in 1947. In 1955, Hussey became dean of Chichester Cathedral, where further artistic commissions included Bernstein's *Chichester Psalms* (1965) and stained glass by Marc Chagall (1887–1985). Mathias's *Missa Brevis* was not actually commissioned by Hussey, but the musical tradition and cultural heritage into which Mathias's Mass must be placed is still very much alive.

The dialogue between celebration and humility that we find in his *Gloria* is symptomatic of faith and worship. We cannot be jubilant with celebration all the time, not only because it is not in our human nature to be so, but also because it is not appropriate.

For while there is much to celebrate in the birth, life, ministry, death, and resurrection of our Lord, bringing hope and salvation, there is also time and place for lament, penitence, and quietude. The Gloria is such a super hymn of praise because it gives a place to these spiritual dimensions in a brief space, and effectively turns even penitence and sorrow for sin into praise. For whether we bring glad rejoicing or pain of sorrow into our worship, both are fit to place at the throne of grace, where Christ crucified and risen presides over all our lives in merciful, loving glory.

God of mercy, you bless us with the ability to praise and glorify your name. Whether we lift our hearts in joy or bow our heads in pain or shame, give us grace to sing of your glory each and every day. Amen.

10. Thomson • *Credo* from
Mass for Two-Part Chorus and Percussion
CD Track 10—4:10

Credo in unum Deum, Patrem omnipotentem, factorem caeli et terrae, visibilium omnium, et invisibilium. Et in unum Dominum Jesum Christum, Filium Dei unigenitum. Et ex Patre natum ante omnia saecula. Deum de Deo, Lumen de lumine, Deum verum de Deo vero. Genitum, non factum, consubstantialem Patri: per quem omnia facta sunt. Qui propter nos homines, et propter nostram salutem descendit de caelis. Et incarnatus est de Spiritu Sancto ex Maria Virgine: Et homo factus est. Crucifixus etiam pro nobis: sub Pontio Pilato passus, et sepultus est. Et resurrexit tertia die, secundum Scripturas. Et ascendit in caelum: sedet ad dexteram Patris. Et iterum venturus est cum gloria, judicare vivos et mortuos: cuius regni non erit finis. Et in Spiritum Sanctum, Dominum, et vivificantem: qui ex Patre Filioque procedit. Qui cum Patre et Filio simul adoratur, et conglorificatur: qui locutus est per Prophetas. Et unam sanctam catholicam et apostolicam ecclesiam. Confiteor unum baptisma in remissionem peccatorum. Et exspecto resurrectionem mortuorum. Et vitam venturi saeculi. Amen.

I believe in one God, the Father Almighty, Maker of heaven and earth, and of all things visible and invisible: And in one Lord Jesus Christ, the only-begotten Son of God, begotten of his Father before all worlds; God of God, Light of Light, very God of very God; begotten, not made; being of one substance with the Father, by whom all things were made: Who for us men, and for our salvation, came down from heaven, and was incarnate by the Holy Ghost of the Virgin Mary, and was made man, and was crucified also for us under Pontius Pilate: He suffered, and was buried: And the third day He arose again, according to the Scriptures, and ascended into heaven, and sitteth on the right hand of the Father: and He shall come again with glory, to judge both the quick and the dead: whose kingdom shall have no end: And I believe in the Holy Ghost, the Lord and Giver of life, Who proceedeth from the Father and the Son, who with the Father and the Son, is worshipped and glorified: who spake by the prophets. And I believe one, holy Catholic and Apostolic Church; I acknowledge one baptism for the remission of sins; and I look for the resurrection of the dead, and the life of the world to come. Amen.

Text: The Nicene Creed
Music: Virgil Thomson (1896–1989) from *Mass for Two-Part Chorus and Percussion*

We now turn to the Credo: the Nicene Creed, which has been said or sung at Eucharists on Sundays and other holy days since at least the fifth century. Not only is the creed a sign of a common belief, it is also an expression of faith in and commitment to God revealed in Father, Son, and Holy Spirit. The history of the creed carries us back to the baptisms of new Christians in Jerusalem. Still today, children or adults are baptized immediately after a profession of the faith. New believers (originally known as *catachumens*) learned church doctrines (a teaching process known as *catechism*) in preparation for baptism; they were exorcized, and immediately before baptism, recited a creedal statement. Baptisms were usually at Eastertide (after a Lenten preparation period) and took place outside the main part of the church. Subsequently fonts were placed in baptisteries (as in Florence), and more often inside the church, at the west end of the building. This tradition is significantly visible in older European churches, and modern churches often

follow that convention today. The font is at the west end because
one could not proceed into the rest of the building without having
been baptized as a Christian, and in order to do that one had to
profess the faith of the creed.

The Nicene Creed carries us straight back to the Council of
Nicea convened by the Emperor Constantine in 325. The purpose
was to counter heresy, especially that of Arius, who denied that
Christ is God. Guided by Athanasius, the Council of Nicea rallied
around a creedal statement that emphasized the inseparability of the
Father and the Son. The creed that we recite or sing today, and that
Virgil Thomson set to music, is not quite the same as this creed from
Nicea. Nowadays we have an extended version, properly called the
Niceno-Constantinopolitan Creed. Slightly altered at the Council of
Constantinople in 381, the revisions were noted at the Council
of Chalcedon in 451.

The creed has traveled with men and women of faith through
many centuries and, as a crucial part of the Mass, inspires composers
in every generation. The American composer and music critic Virgil
Thomson wrote a rather unusual Mass setting for two-part chorus
and percussion in 1934, commissioned by the American League
of Composers and first performed in New York City on April 10,
1935, by the Adesdi Choir of the Dessoff Chorus. Brought up as
a Baptist, Thomson's musical soul was so imbued with hymnody
that many of his works have a hymnodic base. But while he was a
"son of the hymnal" (as fellow composer Leonard Bernstein put it),
he was a sophisticated and technically brilliant composer. He drew
on nineteenth-century popular music, but also broke the rules by
employing open fourths and fifths. While much of his music is tonal
(written more or less in particular melodic keys), at the end of his
Missa Pro Defunctis (Requiem), he uses a twelve-note sequence in
the style of Schoenberg.

The *Percussion Mass* is, not surprisingly, fundamentally
rhythmical. Cymbals and drums are used in the Mass, which in total
is barely twelve minutes long. The *Credo* itself must be one of the

shortest in the repertoire, lasting just four minutes. The first minute and a half contains side drum punctuation of the Latin text sung by the two-part choir with a flowing melody that hints at plainsong. Then the mood changes to a funereal drumbeat on the words *Crucifixus etiam pro nobis* ("He was crucified"). The lower part is like a walking bass, and there is a meandering effect before the *et resurrectio*: the statement of faith in Christ's resurrection, which is more lively. The music becomes more joyful, with a persistent drumbeat building up and receding, adding interest to the relatively speedy singing of the creedal text. The final section has snare drum rolls, which give the conclusion a military feel.

Reciting or singing the creed is something that punctuates our liturgies and our lives. From cradle to grave, we repeat the creed and while we grow and change, it does not, any more than our Lord and Savior, Jesus Christ, changes. The rhythm of the creed sets a drumbeat on our march of faith, which itself is punctuated by the finite beats of our hearts, counting down to the final day when the rhythm stops and we are drawn into the greater harmony of heaven.

God, we believe. Help our unbelief and unite us in the profession of our shared faith, that the beats of our hearts may reverberate in celebration of the story of salvation revealed in your creative power, your saving Son and your loving Spirit. Amen.

11. Lassus • *Sanctus* from *Missa Super Bella Amfitrit' Altera*

CD Track 11—1:29

Sanctus, sanctus, sanctus
Dominus Deus Sabaoth.
Pleni sunt caeli et terra gloria tua.
Hosanna in excelsis.

Holy, holy, holy Lord
God of power and might.
Heaven and earth are full of your glory.
Hosanna in the highest.

Text: Propers of the Mass—Sanctus
Music: Orlande de Lassus (1532–94) from *Missa Super Bella Amfitrit' Altera*

The Sanctus is an ancient hymn of adoration, derived from the prophet Isaiah's vision of angels praising God in heaven: "I saw the Lord sitting on a throne, high and lofty; and the hem of his robe filled the temple. Seraphs were in attendance above him; each had six wings: with two they covered their faces, and with two they covered their feet, and with two they flew. And one called to another and said: 'Holy, holy, holy is the LORD of hosts; the whole earth is full of his glory.' The pivots on the thresholds shook at the voices of those who called, and the house filled with smoke. And I said: 'Woe is me! I am lost, for I am a man of unclean lips, and I live among a people of unclean lips; yet my eyes have seen the King, the LORD of hosts!'" (Isaiah 6:1–5).

Appended to the end of the angels' song is the Hebrew word *Hosanna*. It means "please save us" and is most associated with Jesus' triumphal entry into Jerusalem on Palm Sunday: "So they took branches of palm trees and went out to meet him, shouting, 'Hosanna! Blessed is the one who comes in the name of the Lord— the King of Israel!'" (John 12:13).

Utterly biblical as it is, the Sanctus is generally interspersed between the saying or singing of the first part of the Communion prayer, where God is praised for having created us and sent us Jesus Christ (known as the Eucharistic preface), and the narrative of the institution of Holy Communion (the story of how, at the Last Supper, Jesus took, blessed, broke and shared bread and wine, saying, "This is my body, this is my blood"). In the Eastern church, the Sanctus was in use by the fifth century and the Roman West soon followed suit. The Roman rites became the basis of modern English language liturgies, as revised by the sixteenth-century reformers. While there have been historical changes to the positioning, and even the inclusion of the Benedictus, which often immediately follows the Sanctus, the Sanctus itself has largely remained intact and in this position throughout liturgical history.

It is strange and wonderful to think that what for Isaiah was a cause of fear and trembling, is now for us a regular hymn of praise said or sung daily or weekly at Eucharistic celebrations. Since the coming of Christ, we are able to join "with angels and archangels" in the eternal song of heavenly praise. With the opening up of the kingdom of heaven by Christ, we too have access to the throne of grace, and our communion is not only with each other, but with saints and angels in the presence of God, where "holy, holy, holy" is their song. No doubt they sing it better than we do, but it has to be humbly admitted that there have been some beautiful and sublime efforts made by composers over the years to emulate and encapsulate the music of heaven.

One such composer was Orlande de Lassus (also known as Orlando di Lasso). In spite of his name, Lassus was in fact Flemish, born in Mons, near Hainaut. Spurious legends state that he was a choirboy there and was thrice abducted for the beauty of his voice! We do know, however, that at age twelve he went to work for the

Mantuan Gonzaga family, thereby beginning the Italian part of his career. By 1553, he was *maestro di cappella* (master of chapel music) at the prestigious church of St. John Lateran in Rome. In 1556, he moved to Munich, appointed as a tenor singer by Duke Albrecht V of Bavaria. Although the reformation was at its height in Europe at this time, Lassus remained a Roman Catholic, but tried not to involve himself with ecclesiastical politics. Concentrating on music, he composed settings for services such as Vespers and Mass. It was also his job to educate the choirboys. Lassus became a famous composer, ennobled by kings and popes alike. Lassus married, and two of his sons, Ferdinand and Rudolph, also became musicians and succeeded him in his post, as did his grandson.

He wrote the eight-voice *Missa Super Bella Amfitrit' Altera* in 1610, and drew its musical inspiration from a madrigal, *Bella Amfitrit' Altera*, which, unfortunately, no longer exists. The very brief *Sanctus* opens with a five-note ascending phrase leading us, as up a ladder, into the heights of a rich sound world, in which the text becomes a vehicle for luscious harmony. It can be no coincidence that Lassus begins with a brief ascending scale that then drops back to the starting note, as if to remind us that while we raise our praise to the height of heaven, we are nevertheless grounded on earth. The music gains in intensity and depth as voices enter, taking up the song (listen for the individual entries of "sanctus"), and then the fullness of the sound is underlined by the words *pleni sunt caeli* ("heaven is full"). Then the "hosanna" leaps in, leading to a joyful final cadence. In ninety short seconds, we have been welcomed into the realms of heaven and have caught an aural glimpse of angels in praise.

Multilayered lines of music weave together in what is called counterpoint. Musical counterpoint contributes to the harmony of many-voiced music, involving the beautiful interplay of related yet potentially conflicting melodies. In a sense counterpoint mirrors life, in which the many voices of worldly values, or the unbalancing of compassion, kindness, humility, patience, gratitude, or wisdom can lead to damaging dissonances. If these go unchecked, they can lead to breakdowns in relationships, communities, and societies. As in music, is it perfectly possible for apparently incompatible attitudes or ways of life to blend together, so long as there is a spirit of tolerance such that all can be ultimately harmonized and resolved. Therein lies not only the beauty of contrapuntal music, but also the glorious diversity of the human condition.

Holy and immortal God, give us a pure heart and a simple faith to praise your name and sing your glory. Touch our lips with the fire of your Spirit that we may worship you with confidence and hope, assured always of your mercy and care. Amen.

12. Monteverdi • *Benedictus* from *Missa "In illo tempore"*

CD Track 12—1:25

Benedictus qui venit in nomine Domini.
Hosanna in excelsis.

Blessed is he who comes in the name of the Lord.
Hosanna in the highest.

Text: Propers of the Mass—Benedictus
Music: Claudio Monteverdi (1567–1643) from *Missa "In illo tempore"*

In 1613, the forty-six-year-old Monteverdi assumed one of the most prestigious musical appointments in Renaissance Italy: *maestro di cappella* of St. Mark's Basilica in Venice. At the time, he was master of the court chamber music for Duke Vincenzo Gonzaga of Mantua and was already well-known through his opera *Orfeo* (1607), his madrigals, and some church music published in 1610. In that year, he had also composed his now-famous *Vespers for the Blessed Virgin*, and it is extremely likely that a performance of that setting at St. Mark's on the Feast of the Assumption (August 15, 1613) secured him the illustrious post.

The *Vespers*, like *Orfeo*, broke new ground in a world where older styles were highly valued. Pope Paul V (1550–1621, pope from 1605) was particularly fond of polyphony as exemplified in the work of Palestrina, and Monteverdi wanted to demonstrate his musical versatility when he offered the pope his six-voiced Mass. Intended to be sung without any accompaniment (except an optional *continuo* bass part to keep everyone in tune), the Mass music was based on the motet *In illo tempore*, published in 1554 by the Flemish composer Nicholas Gombert (c. 1495–c. 1560). Gombert was a star of his day, highly rated, but with a colorful past, having served as a galley slave as punishment for molesting children. Gombert earned his pardon by writing beautiful music.

Monteverdi took the musical themes of Gombert's motet, and in homage to him and deference to the polyphony-loving pope, he produced a forty-minute setting of the propers of the Mass as a vehicle to display his own abilities to blend the old and the new. The musical style is archaic and austere and makes us look back half a century over Monteverdi's shoulders, yet Monteverdi's inventiveness and technical skill ushered in a new and breathtaking mastery of old-school polyphony. There is a sense in which this Mass setting is the final step for Monteverdi before he enters into a new compositional world of word-painting and emotional expression.

The polyphonic (many sounding) or contrapuntal style, which Monteverdi used, involves layers of sound, where each melody weaves its way independently of the others. The melodies that are heard in counterpoint are not distinctively different from each other; indeed, the texture of sound is built up by using the same melody in successive voices, turned upside down (inverted) or even sometimes reversed (retrograde). In four- or six- or eight-part choral writing, written for a choir of men and boys, the closeness of harmony and pitch created a mellifluous and rich sound effect. Due to the rules of counterpoint, which forbade consecutive progressions a fifth or a fourth apart (for example), and specified that a melodic line should be played through more or less unaltered (except when avoiding the breaking of the consecutive rules), there were often some interesting and "scrunchy" suspended notes, false resolutions of chords, and even occasional dissonances. It is these that add a distinctive flavor to the otherwise mellifluous nature of polyphony.

There is a sense in which the Eucharist is a polyphonic event. Many strands weave through the account of the Last Supper that we still relate, and yet they are united as they remind us of the sacrifice and love Christ showed in his obedience to his Father's will and desire for humankind.

The part of the Mass known as the Benedictus follows the Sanctus directly and immediately precedes the institution narrative: the part of the Eucharistic prayer in which the celebrant recalls the Last Supper at which Jesus first associated the offering of himself with bread and wine. (This Benedictus is not to be confused with the text from Luke 1:68–79, the thanksgiving uttered by Zechariah when John the Baptist was born.) The Benedictus is invariably found in Latin settings of the Mass (but not always in English ones) and is a quotation from the account of Jesus' Triumphal Entry into Jerusalem: "The crowds that went ahead of him and that followed were shouting, 'Hosanna to the Son of David! Blessed is the one who comes in the name of the Lord! Hosanna in the highest heaven'" (Matthew 21:9).

These are the words called out by the palm-waving crowd when Jesus entered on a donkey, a humble king, yet who was soon to disappoint them. Within days they would abandon him to his fate at the hands of the chief priests and Roman authorities, who would dispose of him quickly and ruthlessly as an inconvenient, rabble-rousing threat to the religious and political status quo.

A text that recollects Palm Sunday is appropriate for a Eucharist. In a sense, Holy Week is acted out in microcosm at every Eucharist: we recall God's creative and saving acts, often referred to in the preface, then we join with angels and archangels in singing "Holy, Holy, Holy," and then acclaim Christ in the Benedictus before locating ourselves in the midst of the central sacrifice of Jesus, offered once and for all on the cross.

When set to music, the strands of polyphony weave together creating a greater whole, each part independent, but each following the rules to create a tight bond of sound, exhibiting and expressing the mercy and love of God, and reminding us of our spiritual journeys that are both individual and corporate. Each musical part, woven in fellowship with the others, makes its own journey, finally arriving at a unified chord, toward which it has striven throughout. While each has its part to play in the whole, each is different, making up a greater body. There is much wavering, some discord even, but all is held together by a common purpose, and when the piece comes to its inevitable conclusion, all is resolved in glory and praise of Jesus Christ who still comes among us in the name of our Father God whenever we break bread together in his name. So it is to him we sing today: *Hosanna in excelsis!*

God of sound and space, who creates and holds us together with bonds of love, guide and guard us as we weave our way on life's pilgrimage, so that when we reach our ultimate destination we may be made worthy to sing Hosannas in your blessed and holy presence. Amen.

13. Rheinberger • *Agnus Dei* from *Mass in E-flat*
CD Track 13—4:08

Agnus Dei qui tollis peccata mundi: miserere nobis.
Agnus Dei, qui tollis peccata mundi: miserere nobis.
Agnus Dei qui tollis peccata mundi: dona nobis pacem.

Lamb of God, you take away the sins of the world,
  have mercy on us.
Lamb of God, you take away the sins of the world,
  have mercy on us.
Lamb of God, you take away the sins of the world,
  grant us peace.

Text: Propers of the Mass—Agnus Dei
Music: Joseph Gabriel Rheinberger (1839–1901), from Mass in
E Flat, op. 109.

The concluding part sung in the musical drama that unfolds in the Mass is the Agnus Dei. The text is based on John the Baptist's exclamation: "Here is the Lamb of God who takes away the sin of the world" (John 1:29, 36). Originally used in Eastern Eucharistic rites, in the seventh century the Syrian Pope Sergius introduced it into the Roman rite as a prayer to be said or sung when receiving the sacrament. Originally it was sung just as the priest broke the bread of Communion, but a tradition evolved that it was to be sung three times, with the final line being changed slightly as a prayer for personal peace. As with the Benedictus, Archbishop Cranmer, in translating and reforming the liturgy for the newly created Church of England in 1549, first included this Communion anthem, but omitted it in the much more Protestant Prayer Book of 1552. It has only been restored in recent years, but now transcends ecumenical divisions.

Joseph Rheinberger, who was born in Vaduz, Lichtenstein, was a Roman Catholic, who displayed a musical talent from the age of five when he began to play the organ. At age seven, he was appointed organist in his parish church in Vaduz and a year later wrote his first Mass setting. At age nine, he studied harmony, and in 1851 was sent to Munich in order to further his education. A contemporary of Johannes Brahms (1833–97), he remained in Bavaria for the rest of his life as organist, teacher, professor at the conservatory, and renowned conductor. When he died in 1901, he had become famous, having had many honors conferred upon him. His grave in Munich was destroyed during the Second World War, so in 1950 his body was returned to Vaduz, where he now rests in peace.

Musically, he was generous-spirited toward innovation, but felt more at home with the baroque and classical masters: Bach, Handel, Mozart, and Beethoven. His music owes them a debt, as it also does to Monteverdi and Palestrina, but his own talent for compositional integrity, watertight structure, and mastery of harmony and counterpoint is evident. Nowadays, he is most revered by organists and choirmasters, who relish his choral output and organ sonatas. He wrote twelve Masses, of which the setting for eight-part choir dedicated to Leo XIII (pope between 1878–1903) and from which this Agnus Dei is taken is probably the most popular and famous.

The Agnus Dei rounds off any musical setting of the Mass, but also brings us back to the beginning in a sense. Eucharists begin with the Kyrie eleison: "Lord, have mercy," and end with the same appeal: "Have mercy on us." The Mass begins and ends with the same appeal to God's mercy, on which we depend. Thus we are reminded of the continuing journey of forgiveness of which our earthly pilgrimages are made. As we strive to walk in the light and love of Christ, assured of his merciful redemption, we also focus much of our devotion on our daily need of God's forgiveness. The Eucharist locates us in prayer and penitence, for bread and wine serve as both spiritual and physical sustenance, both of which we need. Most people do not attend a Eucharist daily, but there is much to be said for a regular and worshipful encounter with Christ in bread and wine. This encounter is a source of remembrance of his saving grace; a source of spiritual sustenance, and a source of fellowship with all those others in different times and places who share, have shared, and who will share communion with us.

The specific words of the Agnus Dei remind us of the corporate nature of our prayer. In the Eucharist much is done from the standpoint of *we*: "We praise you" in the Gloria; "We believe" in the creed; "Have mercy upon us" in the Kyrie, creed, and Agnus Dei; and finally, in the closing words of the Agnus Dei we sing or say, "Grant us peace." When we partake, we are in communion with countless saints and angels celebrating Christ's passion, death, and resurrection, all wrought for us. The fellowship of communion extends beyond our own place and time, and the music, as well as the text, reminds us of this as we hear and sing what our ancestors sang. They lived in a different world, yet worshiped in the same liturgical context. Like us they were sinners but found forgiveness. Gathered around the Lord's Table, we are joined with all who have loved and served Jesus in this and every age.

Rheinberger's double-choir, unaccompanied setting of the Agnus Dei is impassioned, authentic, and tender. We can clearly hear an emphasis on the word *miserere* (mercy), for Rheinberger understands and means what he is setting to music. Unlike some masses by, for example, Bach, or even Copland, Rheinberger's setting, although modern, is clearly intended for liturgical use. His plea for mercy, uttered twice to the Lamb of God, is followed by a restful ending, which not only seeks peace, but illustrates it, as if to acknowledge that those who ask receive: "Ask, and it will be given you; search, and you will find; knock, and the door will be opened for you. For everyone who asks receives, and everyone who searches finds, and for everyone who knocks, the door will be opened" (Luke 11:9–10). So it is with God's mercy: we need only seek it, and we will discover the reward of inner peace. Amen: Let it be so.

Father of mercy and grace, grant to us your servants the inner peace that only your Spirit can sustain, won for us through the saving death and resurrection of your Son, our Lord Jesus Christ. Amen.

14. Esquivel • *Ego sum panis vivus*
CD Track 14—2:08

Ego sum panis vivus qui de caelo descendi: si quis manducaverit ex hoc pane, vivet in aeternum. Alleluia.

"I am the bread that came down from heaven . . . the one who eats this bread will live forever." Alleluia.

Text: John 6:41, 58
Music: Juan Esquivel de Barahona (c. 1563–1614)

In these famous words, Jesus describes himself as the spiritual equivalent of essential and universal food. As "bread of life," he likens himself to a simple and necessary, even vital, foodstuff. "Bread" is not just bread, as it were, it also means "archetypal food," and so he is offering himself as a basic need, such that without him, without "eating" him, we starve spiritually. There is also a sense in which we starve physically. For all food comes from God, as we learn from the book of Genesis: "See, I have given you every plant yielding seed that is upon the face of all the earth, and every tree with seed in its fruit; you shall have them for food. And to every beast of the earth, and to every bird of the air, and to everything that creeps on the earth, everything that has the breath of life, I have given every green plant for food" (Genesis 1:29–30).

Logically we must also conclude that if everything comes from our creator God, then so must our food. There is a sense in which Christ is the bread of life physically as well as spiritually: Christ, at one with God, is literally the provider. He provides food for both physical and spiritual survival, and he also declares that he *is* that food. Even before the incarnation, before his miraculous ministry and before the Last Supper, Christ is already both Word of God and Bread of Life. John gives us this as he opens his Gospel: "In the beginning was the Word, and the Word was with God, and the Word was God. He was in the beginning with God" (John 1:1–2). And it is not long before John also tells us that Jesus is the Bread of Life. Both are key dimensions of our salvation, linked inextricably together: Christ as Word and as sacrament. Our liturgies of preaching and of Eucharist usually involve both, as we join together as the church to hear the Word of God, made flesh in Christ, and to eat his flesh and blood in the bread and wine of Holy Communion. In this way we are truly nourished, for when we eat bread, we consume the means to physical salvation, and when we "eat" Communion, we consume the stuff of spiritual rejuvenation.

If we separate Word and sacrament, we realize how connected they are. Imagine only sharing Communion, but never hearing or reading the Bible! Imagine just reading the Bible and never partaking in Holy Communion! Either approach would be odd, and any Christian behaving in such a way would be impoverished spiritually and might even risk the accusation that they were not true disciples. Concerning the Eucharist, Jesus commands us to "do this in remembrance of me" (Luke 22:19), and St. Paul entreats us to study the Scriptures diligently and regularly: "Give attention to the public reading of scripture, to exhorting, to teaching" (1 Timothy 4:13), for "all scripture is inspired by God and is useful for teaching, for reproof, for correction, and for training in righteousness" (2 Timothy 3:16). Ecclesiastical history reveals times and places where the emphasis on Word or sacrament has changed or been exaggerated, but none of the excesses of Protestant or Catholic piety completely ignored one or the other. While the question as to what the bread and wine *becomes* has influenced modern history irrevocably, producing a steady flow of human blood of its own, the sacrament itself has always been seen and received as a life-giving, positive way of engaging with and receiving a blessing of the promise of salvation revealed in Christ himself. Whatever disagreements may arise as to what the bread of Communion *is*, and how it becomes so, few would dispute that it is the "Bread of Life."

When Esquivel was writing music for the various Spanish cathedrals of which he was the *maestro di capilla* (Oviedo, Calahorra, and then Ciudad Rodrigo), the Catholic doctrine of Holy Communion was well established. The major Eucharistic doctrine of the church drew on the idea of transubstantiation promulgated by Thomas Aquinas (c. 1225–74). Drawing on the thought of Aristotle, Aquinas held that there could be a sense in which the bread and wine retained all the obvious appearances of bread and wine, but were essentially changed through the ministry of the priest into substances that could be truly thought of as Christ's body and blood. This doctrine enhances the mystery, not only of the bread and wine themselves, but of the actions and rituals that accompany or even effect their transubstantiation.

When Esquivel wrote *Ego sum panis vivus* for Pedro Ponce de León, bishop of Ciudad Rodrigo, sometime between 1605 and 1608, this doctrine lay at the heart of Eucharistic and musical theology. The bishop was Esquivel's patron, and paid for the publication of three sets of his motets, in the second of which, *Motecta festorum et domenicarum* ("Motets for Festivals and Sundays") published in 1608, was *Ego sum panis vivus*. The music itself enabled the doctrine to be expressed during Communion in a beautiful way that transcended the simple words of Christ. The beauty of singing evoked the heavenly choirs of saints and angels joining in the eternal banquet, and the ethereal atmosphere produced as bread-become-body was elevated at the crucial moment in the Mass must have been sublime. Augustine once said that "he who sings prays twice," and the use of music to assist the adoration of the Holy Sacrament added a dimension that only music can give. No wonder such music has survived the ups and downs of reformation and theological debate: for it speaks to us on levels that transcend discussion and debate, transporting us to the heavenly realm, where truth and beauty are not uttered, but felt.

Incarnate Christ, Bread of Life, you took our nature and offered yourself as spiritual food so that we might come to know you in your physical resurrection, be a real presence in our lives, to lead us into the beauty and truth of your living way. Amen.

15. Palestrina • *Miserere nostri, Domine*
CD Track 15—3:44

Miserere nostri, Domine, quia multum repleti sumus despectione, quia multum replete est anima nostra: opprobrium abundantibus et despectio superbis.

Have mercy upon us, O LORD, . . . for we have had more than enough of contempt. Our soul has had more than its fill of the scorn of those who are at ease, of the contempt of the proud.

Text: Psalm 123:3–4
Music: Giovanni Pierluigi da Palestrina (1525–94)

Most pieces of music that have the title *Miserere* (such as Gregorio Allegri's famous composition written for use in the Sistine Chapel) are settings of Psalm 51, and are much longer than this delicate short work based on the second half of Psalm 123 by the great Italian composer Palestrina. The word *miserere* has overtones in English: *Miserere nostri, Domine* ("Have mercy on us, O Lord") hints at misery, a word we hardly associate with mercy these days, and yet the English word is derived from the Latin. In old English litanies (responsive sets of prayers often said or sung on Good Friday or other days of penitence), we find the phrase "Have mercy upon us miserable sinners." This does not mean that we are unhappy in general, nor even that we are particularly unhappy about our sinfulness. It means that we are people in need of mercy, and are therefore to be pitied, most of all by God, to whom in Christ we make our plea. In the first eight lines of the litany, the phrase "us miserable sinners" is repeatedly used: to emphasize guilt, and to remind us of our need for mercy.

In Psalm 123 the penitent is also miserable. They have been sated with contempt and scorn, presumably from those who despise or ignore the holy ways of God. The preceding two verses run: "To you I lift up my eyes, O you who are enthroned in the heavens! As the eyes of servants look to the hand of their master, as the eyes of a maid to the hand of her mistress, so our eyes look to the LORD our God, until he has mercy upon us" (Psalm 123:1–2). Thus the "miserable sinner" looks to God for relief, mercy, and restoration. There may well be an underlying connection between one's sin and the contempt of others. Again the psalmist writes: "Deliver me from all my transgressions. Do not make me the scorn of the fool" (Psalm 39:8).

There is irony in this text where Palestrina is concerned, for in his lifetime he had to contend with the deliberations of the papal Council of Trent, which presumed to make decrees not only on church doctrine and dogma, but also on the state and purpose of ecclesiastical music. Palestrina (whose name is taken from the lovely hill town on the slopes outside Rome where he lived) was the finest exponent of a musical style we call *polyphony*. The word simply means "many sounds together," and polyphony evolved as an elaboration of plainsong (monody). Originally the polyphony would be created by weaving together strands of a familiar plainsong melody; hence a simple tune, through creative variation and manipulation, could become the basis of a major piece of musical art.

We might expect this new approach to plainsong to be popular and beautiful, and it certainly was the latter. In the second half of the sixteenth century, the Reformation was the driving force in Northern Europe, with major changes having taken place in Germany, Switzerland, and England, where Protestant theology had replaced the long-held grip of papal influence. Meanwhile, the Roman Catholic Council of Trent was debating the use of music in worship. While Luther was writing hymns, Rome was debating the use of polyphony. Many were advocating its abolition, for they felt that it was obscuring the words: rendering the text incomprehensible. While the reformers were translating the Mass into the vernacular, the popes were demanding that the Latin text be more clearly heard.

Since Palestrina was in charge of music in various papal chapels, the debate about polyphony was raging around him, and was to some extent threatening his livelihood and job satisfaction. Able to write glorious polyphony, he was under threat of having his life's vocation banned. We might wonder whether the words of Psalm 123 had any particular resonance as those who were far less musically informed and competent than himself poured scorn on the style he had perfected. He might well have wondered what he had done to deserve it.

It is both easy and difficult for us to appreciate the significance of the debate over polyphony. It is hard because when we enter the beautiful sound world of Palestrina, we can be transported to another plane on which our encounter with God may be facilitated and nourished. The thought that some people tried to ban this beauty is hard to comprehend. On the other hand, there are still those today who get involved in debates as to what makes appropriate music for worship, and they will sometimes get wound up about it indeed. The question as to which is more important, beauty of music or clarity of text, is still asked: church music, then as now, had the capacity to provoke strong feeling and controversy.

Palestrina was ultimately vindicated and good aesthetic sense prevailed. Within a generation polyphony was so popular and beloved of church leaders that it became known as the "old" style. Music students are required to learn how it works and there are set exercises in polyphonic writing. Palestrina was the father of polyphony, and his musical legacy is still cherished today in his many Masses and motets. Palestrina weathered his fair share of contempt. While we may forget that when we hear his music today, the same beauty of counterpoint may help us remember that while there are always those who are against us, who decry the word and law of God, pouring scorn on our faith, we have a God who in Christ sings a song that resonates and harmonizes with every situation, and brings beauty, truth, and mercy, wherever and whenever we call upon him.

Most merciful Lord, who desires and provides eternal salvation for us, give us strength to resist those who scorn your holy name and restore in us the image of your glory, that returning to the fold of your love, we may always sing your praise. Amen.

16. Handl • *Rorate Caeli*
CD Track 16—2:09

Rorate caeli desuper,
Et nubes pluant justum:
Aperiatur terra et germinet Salvatorem.

Shower, O heavens, from above,
and let the skies rain down righteousness;
let the earth open, that salvation may spring up.

Text: Isaiah 45:8a
Music: Jakob Handl (1550–91)

Jakob Handl was not German, as some suppose, but Slovenian. He was also known as Jacobus Gallus, and possibly Petelin. The three names mean the same thing in German, Latin, and Slovenian: rooster! Born in Ribnica, he became a Cistercian monk at Stina, a fine center of learning since the twelfth century. Around 1565, he moved, first to Melk, a beautiful Austrian Benedictine abbey, and then for ten years he traveled in Moravia, Bohemia, and Silesia, taking a particular interest in the music he encountered. By 1580, he had reached Olomouc in Moravia, where he became choirmaster to the bishop. By 1586, he had been appointed cantor of St. John the Baptist's Cathedral, Prague, a position he held until his untimely death. (The cathedral was destroyed in 1896.)

Handl's anthem *Rorate caeli* was one of his first Prague pieces and was published in *Tomus primus operas musici* (*First Book of Musical Works*) in 1586. It is a luscious piece, involving six voices in close counterpoint. The joyful opening involves a sustained note that leaps up a fifth opening out into quicker notes, which tumble down, portraying the heavens showering from above, and this wavering motif characterizes the whole two-minute piece. The movement is lively and gives a tremendous sense of hopefulness, and of a journey, the destination of which is salvation. The word painting is quite remarkable for a piece of this vintage, and it is certainly striking, even to modern ears.

Handl got the mood right, for although we might approach any request for the coming judgment of God with a certain cautiousness, it is ultimately something to look forward to. Handl's approach is Christian, whereas Isaiah's was not, who had not the return of the Messiah in mind, but his first coming. This is an interesting and often overlooked dimension of Advent, which is itself an oft-forgotten season. There is barely time for a proper celebration of Advent between Thanksgiving and the run-up to Christmas: secular society and commercial demands turn the first half of December into a shopping spree rather than a time of reflection and preparation for the return of our Lord. Advent is not the time when we prepare for Christmas, but the period during which we wait for the Lord. It is a penitential season that blends our attention on the inevitability of judgment, our unfitness to meet our Lord, and the eager anticipation of his return. Such a return inspires not only delight, but also some trepidation, for we all know that when the cool light of judgment is shone upon us, our shadowy souls will be illuminated as we stand ashamed before our God, in whose way of love we have failed to walk. But judgment should not herald despair, for we know God is just, but also loving, and whose nature is to have mercy. So while we stand before him on the last day, both our shame and our redemption, our sorrow and our relief, will be as real as Christ himself: "For we will see him as he is" (1 John 3:2).

Isaiah did not have the benefit of the New Testament, and so his vision pointed his hearers to Christ himself, born of Mary, as Messiah. It is partly for this reason that many misunderstand Advent, because Old Testament prophecy as used in carol services and Advent services points to Christ, rather than to the end of the world. Thus in one sense the fulfillment of Isaiah's prophecies about the coming of a savior is fulfilled in Jesus. Yet while Jesus is the fulfillment of the Old Testament Law and prophecy, his time among us was quite clearly not the end of the world: that is yet to come, and is beheld not only in some of Jesus' own sayings about the end times, but also in the book of Revelation. Fantastical as the end of the world may seem, anyone who understands the basics of solar physics will realize that the end of our planet as a habitable place is not a question of *if* but *when*.

Our solar system is approximately 4.6 billion years old; the sun itself was born from a contracting gas cloud, a genesis that took place a mere ten million years ago. When the temperature in the sun's core reached fifteen million degrees, hydrogen started to burn into helium by a process we call nuclear fusion. This kind of reaction is very stable, and therefore we are living about halfway through this period of the sun's life. After the sun ceases to be stable, it is predicted to become a red giant star so luminous and large that the earth will be engulfed. Finally, apparently long after earth has fried, the sun will die as a compact star: a so-called "white dwarf." We might recall a verse from Mark's Gospel: "The sun will be darkened, and the moon will not give its light, and the stars will be falling from heaven, and the powers in the heavens will be shaken" (Mark 13:24–25).

Human life is a wonder, which we enjoy most of the time. The ability to decide whether we enjoy it is itself a miracle of neuroscience, emotion, behavior, and spirituality. While it is foolish to reject the truths of faith, it is equally foolish to reject the truths of science. But what we, the human race, have learned about our own existence must surely inspire us to trust in God who transcends what we do know and what we do not know, yet loves and sustains us through all the trials and tribulations of the cosmos. He does so by giving us an environment and atmosphere with parameters of survivability that are nothing short of miraculous. One day it will all come to an end in a blaze of glory and power, and all creation shall be redeemed as the heavens open and the skies rain down righteousness.

Open the heavens, O Lord, and pour down upon us the rain of your presence, the thunder of your judgment, and the light of your love, that we may truly believe in, expect, and anticipate the return of your Son, our Lord and Savior Jesus Christ. Amen.

17. Hassler • *Dixit Maria*
CD Track 17—2:36

*Dixit Maria ad angelum: Ecce ancilla Domini, fiat mihi
secundum verbum tuum.*

Mary said to the Angel, "Here am I, the servant of the Lord;
let it be with me according to your word."

Text: Luke 1:38
Music: Hans Leo Hassler (1564–1612)

Mary's acceptance of her call from God as delivered by the angel
is one of the most mysterious but inspiring passages in the
Bible. It gives grace to every carol service and marks the beginning
of the story of the Nativity. It is so well known that we sometimes
overlook the obvious dimensions of salvation that the encounter
and its consequences reveal. Mary says yes to God, affirming her
personal call, and this inspires and challenges us all. In doing so,
she also takes salvation into her own self—she is the first to own the
personal grace and redemption that comes to each one of us through
an acceptance and faith in the Lord Jesus. Mary is the first human
to have and nurture a personal relationship with Christ, who dwells
within her. In this, she is the leader of a multitude, for while her
calling and relationship is unique, it is a model for us all.

We should not forget the obvious, but overlooked, fact that
Christ is conceived and dwells in Mary as an embryo and enters
our realm of sin as an innocent child. It is crucial to some doctrines
of incarnation that Mary is a virgin, precisely to preserve the idea
that the Christ-child is sinless (although this depends on the primary
idea that sex is inherently sinful, an idea that many would dispute
nowadays). Let us not be sidetracked by Mary's virginity, however,

but remember that God comes among us as a child. Mary affirms her own calling and relationship to God in Christ, but God affirms childhood, including it as a major ingredient of the divine plan for redemption. It is significant that Jesus was born, rather than spirited among us in a science-fiction kind of way. We were all children once (even if we can hardly remember it), and God's affirmation of humanity consists not only in the calling of a human mother for his Son, but also in providing for him a full and normal earthly childhood as well as manhood. This also means, of course, that salvation is not necessarily nor exclusively an adult thing, and we need to remember this when engaging with childhood spirituality, prayer, and mission.

The German Renaissance composer Hassler spent his childhood in Nuremberg, but had the most productive period of his musical career in Augsburg, between 1586–1601, where he was a church musician and leader of the town band. In 1604, he moved to Ulm and got married, but moved again in 1608 to Dresden, where he became curator of the extensive musical library there. It was on a trip to Frankfurt with his boss, the Elector of Saxony, that he died of consumption. As well as various Masses and motets, he has left us with the tune of the famous Passion Chorale, used by Bach in the *St. Matthew Passion*, and translated into English as *O Sacred Head, Now Wounded*.

Hassler's setting of Luke 1:38, *Dixit Maria* was written around 1590, and forms part of a collection of motets dedicated to Count Fugger, his employer in Augsburg. It is conventionally polyphonic: four parts enter successively with the phrase *dixit Maria*, appearing first on an F in the tenor, then a fifth above (C) in the altos, then up a fourth (on F again) in the sopranos, and finally, the last entry is by the basses, again commencing on an F. This kind of writing is canonical, parts repeating the same music, but one after another. Much music of the sixteenth and seventeenth centuries employs this technique, which is probably most famously heard in the *Canon* composed by one of Hassler's musical descendants, Johann Pachelbel (1653–1706).

While the structure and style of Hassler's *Dixit Maria* is to some extent formulaic, and we should not read too much into the fact that he used canonical writing to build up a typically Renaissance musical texture, the progress of the music reminds us of the combination of certainty and reflection that Mary must have experienced. Remember the passage from which the text is taken:

And he came to her and said, "Greetings, favored one! The Lord is with you." But she was much perplexed by his words and pondered what sort of greeting this might be. The angel said to her, "Do not be afraid, Mary, for you have found favor with God. And now, you will conceive in your womb and bear a son, and you will name him Jesus. . . ." Mary said to the angel, "How can this be, since I am a virgin?" The angel said to her, "The Holy Spirit will come upon you, and the power of the Most High will overshadow you; therefore the child to be born will be holy; he will be called Son of God. . . . For nothing will be impossible with God." Then Mary said, "Here am I, the servant of the Lord; let it be with me according to your word." (Luke 1:28–31, 34–35, 37–38)

The angel, in visiting Mary, takes her on a swift journey from greeting, through message-giving (the word *angel* means "messenger"), in order to accomplish his mission. It may not be "Mission Impossible," even if it is "Mission Improbable," for Mary's human status gave her the freedom to decline, even if God in his omniscience knew she would accept. The angel's visitation is by no means perfunctory, however, for while the encounter begins with a foreknown yes and ends with a conclusive yes, there is fear and confusion in between. Sometimes polyphonic music can sound confused, meandering, indecisive, yet it not only resolves satisfactorily, but in a way that the end balances the beginning. In polyphony there is an exquisite blend of inevitability and freedom.

Thus Hassler's approach is highly appropriate as a medium for describing the angel's visitation and Mary's inevitable but free acceptance of God's will, not only for her, but also for the whole of creation.

Heavenly Father, whose calling of Mary as mother of your Son affirms the manhood, womanhood, and childhood of humanity, draw each one of us into the inevitability of salvation, but in the freedom of our calling, make us ever worthy of our service in the name of Jesus Christ our Lord. Amen.

18. Nanino • *Adoramus te, Christe*
CD Track 18—2:23

Adoramus te, Christe,
et benedicimus tibi,
quia per sanctam crucem tuam
redemisti mundum.

We adore you Christ,
and we bless you,
because by your holy cross
you have redeemed the world.

Text: Vespers Liturgy for Holy Cross Day (September 14th)
Music: Giovanni Maria Nanino (c. 1543–1607)

Nanino was not a particularly well-known composer, but there is no doubt that he was a fine one. A pupil of the great polyphonic master Palestrina, he succeeded him as chapel music master at Santa Maria Maggiore in Rome, around 1567. In 1577, he became a tenor in the Vatican choir, and it is likely that his setting of *Adoramus te, Christi* was composed during his time there, as the manuscript still exists in the Vatican library.

Nanino's setting is typically polyphonic, higher voices commence, followed by the other voices entering in canonically, that is, singing the same notes, either at the same pitch, or a fourth or fifth above or below. As the piece begins, one can hear the separate entries, before the richer texture of the voices combined makes it harder to discriminate among them. Each part has its own journey to make, but always intersects with the others, sometimes arriving together at a turning point in the text. Polyphonic music, more so than other musical styles, is like a voyage. Each musical line, sung by a differently pitched voice in the choir, starts its own journey through the text, but there is always a harmonious cadence as all the parts reach the same destination together. This makes polyphony very satisfying, for even if there is dissonance along the way, there is resolution and closure at the end. This mirrors the experiences of Passiontide, the Holy Week period, during which Christ was hailed as king on Palm Sunday, but was soon challenged, criticized, betrayed, arrested, flogged, humiliated, and crucified. For Jesus, the way of the Cross was full of dissonance and pain, but its ultimate destination was one of closure for sin and victory over death.

The singing or saying of the brief but profound text of *Adoramus te, Christi* unites us with countless generations who have taken part in what has become known as the Veneration of the Cross. In both Catholic and Protestant churches, many liturgies of Good Friday include these words, either as a response, or as an anthem. On the day when we both lament and celebrate Christ's crucifixion, kneeling at the foot of the cross can be a beautiful and sublime experience, when prayer goes beyond words and the reality of Christ's sacrifice may sink in a little. While the veneration of the cross is generally done in silence, music may precede and follow it, and along with the hymn *Faithful Cross, Above All Other* (to the plainsong *Pange Lingua*), the reproaches and this responsory are often used.

It is also used as a responsorial phrase (the priest speaks the first two lines and the congregation responds) in the walking of the Stations of the Cross. That liturgy often combines readings, music, and movement, as the minister leads the congregation around the church, sometimes outside as well, as a walking of the way of the Cross. In this way the final journey of Jesus from the moment he is condemned to his death on the cross and ultimate resurrection is retold. Often nonbiblical readings are interspersed in what can be a very creative opportunity to engage with Christ's passion, and I know many people for whom it is one of the highlights of the liturgical year, as it enables them to truly enter into the Passion of Christ. The *Adoramus Te, Christi* is so appropriate for these cross-centered occasions, because in a few words it sums up the positive dimension of what would otherwise seem a miserable, bleak event. The Cross of Christ is as much a cause for celebration as for lament. Both dimensions are crucial.

During the medieval period, crosses were commonly seen, and were to be found by the side of roads, at "crossroads" where two roads joined. It was not that the roads intersecting formed a cross, but that a crossroads was where a cross was placed, reminding people of their faith and the journey that life represented. Each turning point provided an opportunity to remember and worship the one who died on the cross. People "signed themselves" with the cross, as many still do, and the cross was marked on them at infant baptism, and indeed, as today, is often found on their coffins. The Christian faith, then as now, was marked by the cross, from font to grave.

The main occurrence of the cross in Nanino's time was to be found in church: the rood cross. *Rood* or *rod* was the name for cross, and it was found on the rood screen, which means "the cross screen," which marked the junction of the people's part of the church (the nave) from the clergy's part (the chancel). Typically, the bottom part of the screen was solid, with panels depicting the saints, while the middle was open, giving sight of the High Altar, and above that, on top was a loft supporting the great rood, the great cross. The cross occupied the central point in the church: the turning point, and the crucifixion was celebrated as the turning point in world history. It truly was the "crux": the crossroads or pivotal point.

Every time we meet Christ on the cross, we arrive at a crossroads, just as medieval pilgrims did. Even now we spend a lot of our time at crossroads of one kind or another. We live on the edge, on the threshold of something, as we make choices and decisions affecting ourselves and others. At the cross, we confront our greatest fear: the fear of death. And yet, in doing so we encounter the complete opposite: we come up close and personal to the gift of eternal life. That is why, ultimately, we are able to adore the

Christ of the cross, rather than hopelessly lament the fact that he was judicially murdered by those who considered him to be a troublemaker. The cross of Christ is a terrible thing, but it is also a wonderful thing, and for that we praise and glorify God in word, movement, and song.

We worship you, Jesus, because by dying for us on the cross you have opened up the path to salvation, eternity, and peace. As we edge toward eternal life, may we take up our crosses for your sake, always turning to your way in trouble and in joy. Amen.

19. Lotti • *Crucifixus*

CD Track 19—2:06

Crucifixus etiam pro nobis; sub Pontio Pilato passus et sepultus est.

He was crucified also for us under Pontius Pilate; he suffered and was buried.

Text: From the Nicene Creed
Music: Antonio Lotti (1666–1740)

There is a tale often told about someone going into a jeweler's shop and asking to buy a silver cross on a chain. The shopkeeper produces a tray of crucifixes of varying sizes, styles, and prices. The customer looks down at the selection, and rather disappointed, asks, "Don't you have any without the little man?"

While most people today know what the cross stands for, there are those who do not. Some that do recognize the cross as a symbol of Christian faith do not quite get the plot, thinking that the figure on the crucifix is no more than a "little man," whose presence is entirely optional in the market economy in which we live and move and have our being.

The Nicene Creed, put together by the ecumenical council that gathered in Nicea in 325 (it's now called Iznik, and is in Turkey), and ratified at the Council of Constantinople in 381, has become the benchmark text for the faith of the church, and it is this small section of the creed, concerning the crucifixion of Jesus, that Lotti sets to music so eloquently. The Council of Nicea was convened to contradict the heresies of Arius, who preached that Jesus was not coeternal with God the Father, but was created by God. This contradicts the belief that Jesus and the Father are part of the same Godhead, making Christ divine. Arius challenged what the church, even in the fourth century, took to be unquestionable, that Jesus was the Son of God, born of the Virgin Mary, who lived among us, was crucified under Pontius Pilate and rose again on the third day.

We might wonder why Pilate gets a mention and a place in history. In spite of his rather unpleasant way of running the Roman province of Judea in Jesus' time and the way in which he disposes of Jesus while getting the Jewish leaders to do all the legwork, Pilate is a useful historical figure, the mention of whom locates and grounds the death of Jesus when it comes to saying or singing the Creed. For his existence is not in doubt: we know that he really existed and was governor of Judea from AD 26 to 36. He is mentioned in association with the death of Jesus by the Roman historian Tacitus, the Jewish historian Josephus, and by the Greek Philo. Pilate existed, and so too did Jesus. No one in their right mind doubts that these two men were in Judea at the same time in the first century, and it is equally implausible to suggest or believe that the crucifixion did not happen. The New Testament and other histories attest to Jesus being crucified under Pontius Pilate. We cannot take Christ off the cross, because historians locate him there. So the question to be asked and considered is not, "Did Jesus exist?" Nor, "Did Jesus die?" but, "What is the significance of Jesus Christ?"

It is the significance of Christ that concerns composers such as Antonio Lotti. For while the text states the bald fact that Christ died under Pilate and was buried, the music tells us far more. For when one listens to Lotti's eight-part motet, there is no doubt of the significance of the death of Christ. The creedal text tells us what to *believe*, but Lotti's music tells us what to *feel*.

Lotti was born in Hanover in the year that the Great Fire destroyed London. Although born in Germany, he was Venetian; his father, Mateo, was a music director in Hanover. His career as a singer and organist culminated in his appointment as *primo maestro di capella* (director of chapel music) at St. Mark's Basilica, Venice, in 1736 (the same post Monteverdi had held a century earlier). One of his tasks in Venice was to write music for the banquets given by the doge. Like Monteverdi, Lotti wrote operas as well as sacred music, and made a good career doing so. He composed many settings of the *Crucifixus* of which this eight-voice version is the best known of all his works today. It comes from a five-movement setting of the creed, in F major, written during a leave of absence in Dresden between 1717 and 1719. Most of the work is in four parts, but the choir divides into eight for this brief but moving section of the creed.

It is not an easy piece to sing, as each of the parts is exposed as it enters successively, moving up from the bass's opening entry. Just as the church grows in faith through the witness of the saints, the sound builds, adding height and width, the musical texture swelling as the statement of fact (*crucifixus*) becomes a foundation of faith (*etiam pro nobis*). Christ was not simply crucified, but what is significant, and heartrending, is that he was crucified *for us*. And when one hears Lotti telling us this, one cannot help but believe it. Such is music's ability to speak, and heal, and convert at levels below and above speech. So by the time we reach *et sepultus est* ("and was buried"), two-thirds of the way into this two-minute piece, we are truly drawn into the emotion of the motet, such that we are truly mourning the death of Christ.

And mourn it we should, sinners that we are, for his death is for us. Yet there can be no crucifixion without resurrection and no resurrection without death. Lotti's piece, sung in isolation, implies that there is death without resurrection. Choirs can be forgiven for singing this glorious music isolated from the text that follows it: *et resurrectio tertia diae* ("and rose again on the third day"), but when we hear this beautiful music draw to an end, let us never forget that the crucifixion and burial describes not the end of the story, but the beginning of the new life opened up for us in Jesus Christ our risen Lord.

Father God, in response to the love and freedom you sent among us in your Son Jesus Christ, our ancestors ignored, bullied, brutalized, and killed him. We confess our part in history yet affirm your saving grace by which his crucifixion buried death and sin for good. By your Spirit, bless us as we constantly call to mind your redeeming love, until that day when we shall see him as he is, in whose dear name we pray. Amen.

20. Tchaikovsky • *Angel vopiyáshe*
CD Track 20—2:48

Angel vopiyáshe Blagodátney: chistaya Dévo, ráduysia; I páki rekú, ráduysia: Tvoy Sïn voskrése tridnéven ot gróba, i mértvïya vozdvígnuvïy, liúdiye, veselítesia!

Svetísia, svetísia, nóvïy Iyerusalíme: Sláva bo Ghospódinia na tebé vozsiyá: likúy nine i veselisia, Sióne! Ti zhe Chístaya, krasúysia Bogoróditse, o vostánii rozhdesvá Tvoyegó.

The angel cried to the lady full of grace: Rejoice, O pure virgin! Again I say: rejoice! Your Son is risen from his three days in the tomb! With himself he has raised all the dead! Rejoice all you people!

Shine! Shine! New Jerusalem! The glory of the Lord is risen upon you! Exult now and be glad O Zion! Be radiant, pure Mother of God, in the resurrection of your son!

Text: From the Orthodox Liturgy for Holy Saturday
Music: Peter Illych Tchaikovsky (1840–93)

Tchaikovsky is possibly Russia's most famous composer, and much of his music is extremely famous. His apparently tormented life, mysterious death, and deeply emotional music lends itself to the art forms with which he is most often associated: ballet and opera. A sensitive man, he was unnaturally gifted in the expression of musical emotion, but which for some is over dramatic, even mawkish. Yet Tchaikovsky is not well known for his liturgical music, such as the *Liturgy of St. John Chrysostom*, written in 1878, or the *Nine Sacred Choruses* of 1884–85. Another chorus, *Angel vopiyáshe*, was written in 1887, but was lost soon after its first performance, only resurfacing thirteen years after Tchaikovsky died.

The text comes from a hymn that is traditionally sung at Easter in the Orthodox Church. It is not drawn from the Bible directly, but is full of scriptural resonances. The opening greeting is reminiscent of the Annunciation, in which Gabriel greets Mary and reveals to her God's plan that she should be the mother of Christ (Luke 1:26– 38). The repeated charge to rejoice is reminiscent of Paul writing to the Philippians: "Rejoice in the Lord always; again I will say, Rejoice" (Philippians 4:4). The news the angel brings is taken from the end of Luke's and Mark's Gospels: "They saw a young man, dressed in a white robe, sitting on the right side; and they were alarmed. But he said to them, 'Do not be alarmed; you are looking for Jesus of Nazareth, who was crucified. He has been raised; he is not here'" (Mark 16:5–6). The second part of the hymn draws its inspiration from Isaiah's words: "Get you up to a high mountain, O Zion, herald of good tidings; lift up your voice with strength, O Jerusalem, herald of good tidings, lift it up, do not fear; say to the cities of Judah, 'Here is your God!' . . . Arise, shine; for your light has come, and the glory of the LORD has risen upon you" (Isaiah 40:9, 60:1). The final line of the text, also directed to the Virgin, is not scriptural, but sums up the feeling of the whole hymn: that of rejoicing in the resurrection of Christ.

In this textual compilation, we are reminded not only of the Easter promise, but of the Resurrection as fulfillment of prophecy, working on various levels. First, as far as Mary is concerned, this is the culmination of all that she has borne in both joy and grief. From the Annunciation, when the angel told her she had a special role to play, through the prophecy of Simeon, who warned her, "This child is destined for the falling and the rising of many in Israel, and to be a sign that will be opposed so that the inner thoughts of many will be revealed—and a sword will pierce your own soul too" (Luke 2:34–35), there is a strand of pain that she bears, pain that reaches a terrible climax at the foot of the cross. To see a son die is a terrible burden of heaviness, and is literally painful, and as she wept on Good Friday, it must have been small comfort to Mary that it was destined to be and would have world-saving consequences. Yet, on the third day there is a different feel as angels proclaim the Resurrection and exclaim, "He is risen." Liturgically speaking, without this kind of hymn for Mary, we are left with the Mary of the *Stabat Mater,* weeping at the cross, desolate that everything is over. This hymn expresses her reason to rejoice, and makes a full circle of her angelic encounters.

Second and more broadly, there is the Resurrection as fulfillment of God's plan to redeem humankind. In Isaiah particularly, we find the figure of the suffering servant, a character often associated with Christ the Messiah, who comes to redeem Israel: to suffer and to die that others might live. So in these words we discover not only a personal dimension involving Mary, but reference to God's wider plan, the sending of the long-awaited Messiah, whose ministry culminates in the Cross, but pushes through to the joyful third day of resurrection, salvation, and glory.

Given these flavors of rejoicing, we might expect Tchaikovsky's music to be exuberant from the start. Yet it is not, and perhaps as such, more accurately reflects the emotional depth of the context in which the words must be seen. Like the transition from sadness to joy that must have bewildered Jesus' mother, Tchaikovsky's setting begins almost sadly, before soaring sopranos remind us of the joyful tidings the angel brings. Central outbursts of joy are appropriate for the Easter season, but subside as the news of resurrection is emphasized. This gentle conclusion might surprise us, for the music does not end on a great chord of joy as we might expect, but rather suggests the contentment and relief of closure that, perhaps for Mary, has finally come. In the culmination and completion of God's saving plan, she and her own beloved Son are both instruments and victims, emotionally and theologically. There is a sense of arrival here, and while the church rightly rejoices annually at Eastertide, it seems that Tchaikovsky has peered into the emotional heart of Mary at the Resurrection and witnessed her delighted but tired heart. Thus, the angel brings her not only glad tidings, but also balm for her soul.

Saving God, give us grace to be your Easter people that we may both see through the pain of the world to the eternal hope that Christ won for all your people; and be evangelists of the same, revealed in the power and glory of his resurrection. Amen.

21. Byrd • *Terra tremuit*
CD Track 21—0:49

Terra tremuit, et quievit, dum resurgeret in Judicio Deus. Alleluia.

The earth trembled and was still, when God arose in judgment. Alleluia.

Text: See Psalm 76:8–9
Music: William Byrd (c. 1540–1623)

William Byrd, who was one of the most prolific and promising organists and composers of his day, published *Terra Tremuit* as Number 23 in his liturgical collection, *Gradualia II*, of 1607. Although it is a pre-Christian psalm text, it is intended for and is appropriate for use on Easter Day, as it reminds us very dramatically of the earthquake that heralds the resurrection: "And suddenly there was a great earthquake; for an angel of the Lord, descending from heaven, came and rolled back the stone and sat on it" (Matthew 28:2). It must be one of the most economical pieces of music ever written, for in less that a minute Byrd paints a word picture of an earthquake shaking the foundations of the world, yet in such a way as to invoke the response "Alleluia." In such a short space of time, we have terror and joy: a wide emotional range expressed in a microcosmic combination of hope and fear.

Earthquakes are not common in the Bible, but when they occur, there is great significance. Lovers of John Greenleaf Whittier's hymn *Dear Lord and Father of Mankind* may remember the story to which the last verse alludes: God's voice is heard by Elijah in the "still small voice of calm," but only after the wind, earthquake, and fire have done their worst (see 1 Kings 19:11–12). For Isaiah, however,

God comes in terrible judgment in the midst of an earthquake and fire (Isaiah 29:6) and the psalmist has this in mind in Psalm 76. At the end of the Bible, the book of Revelation has four separate references to an earthquake heralding the final judgment. The shaking of the heavens and the earth are very much part of most end-time scenarios.

The prophet Amos also uses earthquake imagery to express the judgment of God. It is clear that while we have little specific evidence of tremors around his time, experiences of earthquakes in Israel were very real. But while earthquakes symbolize judgment, they also herald salvation. For Peter in prison, an earthquake causes the foundations to shake, breaking his chains and enabling him to escape (Acts 16:26). A blend of salvation and judgment is found in the earthquake that opens the graves of the faithful departed as Jesus dies on the cross (Matthew 27:53–54), and again at the Resurrection, as we have seen. As the earth literally trembles, judgment and salvation go hand in hand, simultaneous causes of both fear and praise. In that way the psalmist is able to say "Alleluia" in the face of the earth quaking before judgment, and we too can echo it when we contemplate the reality of judgment and salvation brought about in the resurrection of Christ.

Alleluia literally means "praise God," and is derived from the Hebrew word for praise (*halelu*) and the shortened form of *Jahweh*, *Jah*. Ancient as the word is, it is still said and sung with the same meaning and intent as it always has been. In the context of Psalm 76, this means that we praise God for his judgment, even though it is terrifying. Byrd's setting of the text suggests a good balance when it comes to combining fear and trembling with praise: it is not an easy mix, but Byrd's almost literally expressive approach succeeds very well, albeit briefly.

The opening sounds shaky (but must be sung confidently), and is followed by repeated alleluias in the second half of the anthem. Thus the emphasis is on praise rather than fear, and this is entirely appropriate given the spirit of the psalmist's words: yes, he seems to say, there is cause for fear, but greater cause to praise the Lord. The experience of faith is condensed in this musical minute, for while our fear of judgment is ameliorated by the assurance of mercy, at the same time we cannot contemplate salvation without comprehending our unworthiness of such a divine gift.

For the scientist, an earthquake is a naturally occurring phenomenon, the consequence of the plates of the earth's surface sliding up against and on top of one another, causing friction and eventual fracture along the fault lines in the earth's surface. Earthquakes are part of the created order; our planet has tectonic plates, a hard shell on which all life moves and has its being. If the earth did not have such a crust, it is extremely unlikely we could exist. Thus the very ground under our feet, on which we have been placed to dwell, can also be the cause of great destruction to the human race and other life-forms. Rumbling through eons of history, the plates of the earth's surface move with a slow freedom that epitomizes the independence of creation. Similarly, the mutation of cells is a natural process that has caused adaptation and survival of various species, but the same process of mutation also causes cancers to develop.

On a bigger scale, the way God has made the world provides us with an environment conducive to human flourishing, but the freedom embedded in the universe can harm us too. Earthquakes therefore are neither random occurrences, nor God's judgments. Yet they do happen—we cannot prevent them and sometimes suffer from their consequences. They are excellent symbols of God's judgment, because that too will surely happen, cannot be prevented, and, according to prophecy, will not be pleasant for some. Yet we can respond to and be prepared for the inevitability of judgment, just as those in earthquake zones also take precautions. We may feel small and seem insignificant in the face of judgment, but in Christ, there is hope, and protection, and the promise of eternal life to all who turn to him in penitence and faith.

God, our judge and redeemer, shake the earth with your loving mercy and pour your righteousness into the fault lines of our faith. Spare us in the day of tribulation, that we may rise with Christ to eternal life with all the saints. Amen.

22. Mendelssohn • *Am Himmelfahrtstage*

CD Track 22—1:36

Erhaben, O herr, über alles Lob, über alle Herrlichkeit,
herrschest du von Ewigkeit, Hallelujah!

Be raised, O Lord, over all praise, above all splendor, for
you reign throughout all eternity! Alleluia!

Text: Based on 1 Chronicles 29:10–11
Music: Felix Mendelssohn-Bartholdy (1809–47), op. 79

Inevitably, Ascensiontide is associated with heights. In some
churches a firework is lit, ascending heavenward in a flash of light,
celebrating the important feast day with a bang. In some churches,
there is a walk to the top of a local mountain, a journey that makes
a small attempt to get closer to heaven. While mountains give good
physical vantage points, Ascension Day gives us a great spiritual
and liturgical vantage point.

The Ascension of Christ puts us in a splendid position from which
to survey the events of the previous forty days, and in the greater
distance, the forty days that preceded it: the forty days of Easter and
before it, the forty days of Lent. In a sense, on Ascension Day we
can look back over eighty days in which, liturgically speaking, we
truly have traveled great distances. Unlike Jules Verne's ballooning
adventurers, who went *Around the World in Eighty Days*, we have
been around the Word (of God) in eighty days.

Lent begins with the Temptation in the wilderness, preparing us
for the self-denial of Lent, during which we pass Mothering Sunday
and journey into Passiontide. Arriving in Holy Week, we follow the
Way of the Cross, and join in the great *Triduum*: the three days of
Maundy Thursday, Good Friday, and Easter Eve. Then we reach
the Resurrection on Easter Day, sharing with the disciples the Good

News of the risen Lord. But this is only halfway through, for there are forty days of Easter to follow. Luke specifically tells us that Jesus was to be encountered in physical form for forty days after the Resurrection (Acts 1:3), and there are numerous accounts of his being so. Only then, having been "seen among us," did he depart.

This is what happens to us all. We are all "seen among us" for a little while, and then we go hence, yet in spite of the psalmist's appeal in Psalm 39:4 ("Lord, let me know my end, and what is the measure of my days"), we do not know how long we will live. So Jesus' ascension gave his disciples a proper farewell, and it was the nearest thing to a funeral that we can think of for Jesus. His burial was so hurried and in such tormented circumstances that there was a pastoral and psychological need for the disciples to see him ascend to heaven. Yet there is also a sense in which every funeral should be like the Ascension.

For at every Christian funeral there is the promise of resurrection and of hope. Jesus tells his disciples, "If I go and prepare a place for you, I will come again and will take you to myself, so that where I am, there you may be also. . . . I am the way, and the truth, and the life. No one comes to the Father except through me" (John 14:3, 6). Later Jesus ascends, promising the gift of the Holy Spirit, and the same Spirit is with us whenever we gather in his name. When we say farewell to someone at a funeral, there is always the hope of eternal life, not in the background as most of the time, but very much in the foreground.

This is why most musical settings of ascension texts are exuberant and joyful, and Mendelssohn's brief setting of words of praise for Ascensiontide is no exception. He was the grandson of the Jewish thinker Moses Mendelssohn. He added the surname Bartholdy when he converted to Christianity. Born in Hamburg but brought up in Berlin, the young Felix had the benefit of a cultured education. In the early 1830s, he traveled widely for further education, spending time in Italy and Great Britain. He is to be credited with the beginnings of the revival of Bach's music in both Germany and Britain. Like Bach, Mendelssohn was a Lutheran, and although his more romantic, tuneful style is not so like his hero of two centuries earlier, Bach's approach to harmony and counterpoint made a lasting impression.

Mendelssohn's brief anthem, written on October 9, 1846, expresses a postpentecostal attitude to the Ascension, such that we rejoice that Jesus has gone before us to prepare the way of truth and life. Our songs of praise are sung from a spiritual distance and in a different time zone. For the disciples it must have been very different, not as shocking or painful as the humiliation and despair they felt at the crucifixion, but even when beloved friends go to heaven, it is nevertheless distressing, sometimes shocking, to lose them suddenly. Even with forty days' notice this time, the disciples must have felt dejected when they experienced the emotional roller coaster of the fifty-seven days that span the space between Palm Sunday and Pentecost. It began and ended well, euphorically almost, but there were many ups and downs in between. Only at Pentecost did it all make sense, and only then, presumably, did Jesus' friends come to terms with his death and resurrection, being given the internal joy and peace to live and witness in a spirit of hope, salvation, and delight.

We do not have to live through that kind of experience, except perhaps when tragedy strikes our families and friends, in which case the example of the disciples can give some comfort. Generally for us now, it is more natural to treat Ascensiontide as an occasion for rejoicing, and for repeating those words of David, from 1 Chronicles, on which Mendelssohn based his brief anthem: "Yours, O LORD, are the greatness, the power, the glory, the victory, and the majesty; for all that is in the heavens and on the earth is yours; yours is the kingdom, O LORD, and you are exalted as head above all" (1 Chronicles 29:11).

Christ enthroned on high, we celebrate your victory over death and the promise it gives us. Deal graciously with those who mourn, and give us the courage and strength to walk toward heaven with hope in our hearts and praise on our lips. Amen.

23. Philips · *Tibi laus*

CD Track 23—3:16

Tibi laus, tibi gloria, tibi
gratiarum actio in saecula
sempiterna, O beata Trinitas.
Caritas Pater est, gratia
Filius, communicatio Spiritus
Sanctus, O beata Trinitas.
Verax est Pater, veritas Filius,
veritas Spiritus Sanctus, O
beata Trinitas. Pater et Filius
et Spiritus Sanctus una
substantia est, O beata Trinitas;
et benedictum nomen gloriae tua
sanctum, et laudabile, et
superexaltatum in saecula.

To thee be praise, glory, and
thanksgiving for ever, O blessed Trinity.
The Father is love, the Son grace,
and the Holy Spirit imparting, O blessed Trinity.
The Father is full of truth, and the
Son and Holy Spirit are truth, O
blessed Trinity. The Father, the Son,
and the Holy Spirit are of one
substance, O blessed Trinity;
and the holy renown of your glory is
blessed, full of praise, and exalted for ever.

Text: From the antiphon and responsory for Trinity Sunday
Music: Peter Philips (1561–1628)

The life of a chorister at St. Paul's Cathedral is a varied, hard-working, exciting, and privileged one. Boys are auditioned, sometimes aged only six or seven, and if they are deemed to have musical potential, and strength of character to endure the rigors of schooling, living away from home and singing twice daily, six days a week, they become part of the cathedral's ancient musical foundation. Nowadays there are pastoral, practical, and academic safeguards in place, and choristers generally look back on their time as happy, fulfilling, and very special indeed. When they leave, at about age thirteen, they have sung for the Queen, been part of festival services commemorating or commiserating national or international events, and they have acquired a musical education that is unmatched worldwide. Inevitably, boys and girls growing up and learning in any environment have ups and downs, but the situation today is far better than it was in 1574 when the young Peter Philips was a chorister at St. Paul's.

For it wasn't until the nineteenth century that a formidable lady, Maria Hackett, decided to champion the cause of the neglected choirboys, who were poorly paid and given little education and no proper accommodation. As money was short, the boys had to sing at concerts and banquets in the evenings to pay their keep, and were often seen roaming the streets late at night as a consequence. Hackett's campaigning zeal on behalf of the boys never abated, and eventually, in 1876, a cathedral choir school was opened in Carter Lane, near the cathedral. That building is now a youth hostel, the school having subsequently moved.

In Peter Philips's day, therefore, being a cathedral chorister was neither easy nor lucrative. Worse still, it was a dangerous time ecclesiastically. Philips's mentor, Sebastian Westcote, who was in charge of the choirboys at the time, was appointed by the Catholic Queen Mary, and after her death in 1558, Westcote got into a lot of trouble with the restored Protestant authorities. Thus when Westcote died in 1582, Philips had little protection and fled to Rome for refuge.

Nowadays, choristers have a better life and the issues of ecclesiology that divide churches and denominations are far less serious, at least in consequence, if not content. Today, ecumenism focuses on what we share as Christians, and while there are still issues concerning the symbolism and status of the Eucharist, for example, much is widely accepted across denominational divides. A very good example is the belief in God as Trinity: a complex doctrine, inferred from Scripture, that unites all churches in the belief that God is three-in-one, as Father, Son, and Holy Spirit. Peter Philips's setting of *Tibi laus* would not have offended Protestants for its content, although the use of Latin was frowned upon in post-Reformation England. Published in Philips's first major collection, the *Cantiones Sacrae,* Antwerp, 1612, it is in five voices, and as befits a trinity anthem, is in three-quarters time: three beats in a measure, marking out a threefold beat with which to worship the Trinity.

The music begins with only the upper voices singing for the first half minute, and this gives a greater impact to when the men enter, praising, *O beata Trinitas* ("O blessed Trinity"). After a rich central part extolling the unity of the Trinity, there is a final frenetic section in which all the parts sing repeated notes, creating a mood of ecstasy and exuberance as the glory of God is praised, before a satisfying close on an F-major chord. What begins quite peacefully, builds and grows, responding perhaps to the increasing power and mystery of the trinitarian Godhead. This is a joyous piece, which relishes the relationship among Father, Son, and Holy Spirit, and takes delight in our ability to relate to God in this way.

This is an anthem for Trinity Sunday, the Sunday following Pentecost. It is perhaps strange that a doctrine, on which much of the church's faith is built, should have a feast day, rather as a saint or an event might. Christmas and Easter are historical occasions, celebrated amid the seasons of the year, while saints tend to have a festival around the date of some event in their lives, such as birth or martyrdom. Trinity Sunday celebrates a doctrine, and did not find a regular place in the church calendar until the Middle Ages, when Pope John XXII encouraged and commended it. Trinity Sunday was popular in England, and even today in ecclesiastical traditions that are English in origin, the Sundays after Pentecost are counted as "Sundays after Trinity."

The text that Philips sets is derived from the antiphon and responsory for that feast of Trinity, which was used before and after psalms set for the day at either Mass, or an Office Service, and where plainsong was used, one side of the choir might respond to the antiphon, the music thus bounces from one side to another. Philips's setting is not antiphonal in this way, although the delayed entry of the lower voices could create a response and answer acoustic effect in certain buildings. In any event, it is a luxurious, richly textured hymn of adulation to the Godhead, celebrating not only the interrelatedness of Father, Son, and Holy Sprit, but also the saving relationship of grace and redemption that we all enjoy with God the Father, through the Son and in the power of the Holy Spirit.

Holy and eternal God, accept our humble offerings of praise, so that our hearts may feel your fatherly love, our souls be inspired by your Holy Spirit, and our minds filled with the knowledge of Christ, for you reign, Trinity in unity. Amen.

24. Sowerby • *Eternal Light*
CD Track 24—2:23

Eternal light, shine into our hearts,
eternal goodness, deliver us from evil,
eternal power, be our support,
eternal wisdom, scatter the darkness of our ignorance,
eternal pity, have mercy upon us;
through Jesus Christ our Lord. Amen.

Text: Alcuin of York (c. 735–804)
Music: Leo Sowerby (1895–1968)

The eighth-century English deacon whom we have come to call Alcuin was also known as Ealhwine or, in Latin, Flaccus Albinus Alcuinus. While many assume that he was both a priest and a monk, there is no actual evidence to prove he was either, but the spiritual depth of Alcuin's life and writing is clear enough. He studied at the cathedral school in York, and became a teacher there some time around 750. York was, and still is, the second ecclesiastical city of England, the center of the Northern province and in the ancient minster is still the seat, the *cathedra* of the archbishop (Canterbury having the seat of the Southern archbishop, the successor to St. Augustine, and *Primus inter Pares* [first among equals] of the Worldwide Anglican Communion). In 767, Aelred became archbishop of York, and around that time Alcuin was ordained deacon and became the headmaster of the school in York. In 781, Alcuin was sent to Rome by the Saxon King Elfwald, and while there he met the man who was to become known as Charlemagne, the king of the Frankish kingdom. Charlemagne hired Alcuin to teach the princes and the clergy, and this he did for nine years before returning to England for a brief period. By 794, Alcuin was heavily engaged in combating heresy at the Council of Frankfurt, and was

revered and respected as a theologian. Two years later, the abbot of
St. Martin at Tours died and Charlemagne asked Alcuin to replace
him, and he spent the rest of his life there teaching the monks and
advising Charlemagne on theological and spiritual matters.

Written around 804, the last year of his life, this prayer by
Alcuin brings the beauty of eternity into the mundane human
world of sin and frailty, transcending any distinction between
life and death. God the Father is addressed as eternal light,
goodness, power, wisdom, and pity, whose munificence toward us
mere mortals manifests itself as divine illumination, protection,
support, knowledge, and forgiveness. In one short prayer, Alcuin
packs in a collection of virtues and rewards that give us a concise
and inspiring snapshot of our spiritual needs, and the source
from which they are met.

There is little doubt that Alcuin was one of the most significant
ecclesiastical figures of his day, not only because of what he knew,
but in virtue of who he knew. Respected and admired by the
greatest ruler of his age, Alcuin's influence on Charlemagne, and
therefore on contemporary ecclesiastical and political reform,
was significant. Even today, the English society for promulgating
and studying the academic dimensions of church liturgy is
known as the Alcuin Club. If we jump forward a millennium
from Alcuin's day, we find that the composer Leo Sowerby was
similarly revered and respected by the American church musical
world. It may seem strange to compare Alcuin and Sowerby,
but they are linked, not only by this beautiful anthem in which
Sowerby sets Alcuin's prayer, but by their status in the worlds
that they commanded.

Sometimes referred to as the Dean of American Church
Music, Sowerby, like Alcuin, displayed a certain precociousness
in early life. Born in Grand Rapids, Michigan, he began to write
music at age ten, and while he was still a teenager, the Chicago
Symphony Orchestra premiered his violin concerto in 1913. He
subsequently won the prestigious Prix de Rome in 1921 and a

Pulitzer Prize in 1946 for his setting of words by St. Francis of Assisi, the "Canticle of the Sun." In 1927, he became organist and choirmaster at what was to become Chicago's St. James's Cathedral (it was consecrated as such in 1955), and Sowerby remained there until his retirement in 1962. He then spent the final years of his life based at Washington's National Cathedral, where he set up the College of Church Musicians. On his death, he left a large catalogue of compositions, including five symphonies and some chamber music. Yet much of Sowerby's output is sacred music, and it is his church music for which he is mostly remembered and admired.

His peaceful and meditative five-voice anthem *Eternal Light*, written in 1958, enables its hearers to enter into a spirit of prayer, borne along by the ebb and flow of gentle music. The opening is like a little sunrise, depicting the light of Christ, rising to illuminate our prayers, but then the way Sowerby's music follows the text gives an impression of waves lapping on a shore: as each attribute of God is stated, the petition for the divine gift of mercy, understanding, or enlightenment pulls us both away from and toward the next phrase. Sowerby's word setting is clarity itself, and a good choir can easily make each word distinct, further enabling the listener's participation in this musical act of prayer.

Prayer takes many forms, and music has a unique ability to express and embody those forms. Sometimes prayer is fervent, impassioned, even desperate, as pleas for healing, mercy, or deliverance in the face of pain, anger, or fear batter the gates of heaven. At other times prayer is the gifted result of solitude, contemplation, or silence. Sowerby's *Eternal Light* is a musical equivalent of prayer emanating from stillness and love. We are not all naturally inclined to pray like this, nor is it always easy to feel so content in the presence of God, but with music of such beauty and truth as this to aid us, we can try to surrender to its direction and be enabled to ride on the waves of prayer as they lap on the shores of heaven.

God of goodness and mercy, shine the light of your wisdom into our hearts, that, united with your saints in every age, we too may live according to the vision of your glory, and ultimately be drawn into the company of the redeemed, who worship you, Father, Son, and Holy Spirit, now and through all eternity. Amen.

25. Brahms • *Ach, arme Welt*

CD Track 25—2:18

Ach, arme Welt, du trügest mich,
ja, das bekenn ich eigentlich,
und kann Dich doch nicht meiden,
und kann Dich doch nicht meiden.
Du falsche Welt, du bist nicht wahr,
Dein Schein vergeht, das weiss ich zwar,
mit Weh und großem Leiden,
mit Weh und großem Leiden.
Dein Ehr, Dein Gut, Du arme Welt,
im Tod, in rechten Nöten fehlt,
Dein Schatz ist eitel, falsches Geld,
dess hilf mir, Herr, zum Frieden
dess hilf mir, dess hilf mir, Herr, zum Frieden.

Oh, poor world, you deceive me, yes I know that definitely,
And still you are not able to be avoided.
You false world, you are not true,
Your light fades, this I know, with woes and great suffering.
Your hour, your gods, you poor world,
In death, in need they all shall fail.
Your treasure is vain, false gold,
Lord, help me to rejoice.

Text: Heinrich von Laufenberg (d. 1460)
Music: Johannes Brahms (1833–97), op. 110, no. 2, 1889

The words of this motet by the German romantic composer Brahms may strike us as a little odd, for they seem very negative, the product of a mind resentful and despairing of the world. While some commentators say that the text is anonymous, it is likely that the words are by Heinrich von Laufenberg, a fifteenth-century German monk. He was a priest at Freiburg im Breisgau before becoming Dean of the cathedral there, and then joined the Knights of the Order of St. John in 1445. He died in Strasbourg, and although much of his work survived there, most of it was destroyed during the Franco-Prussian War when Strasbourg came under siege in 1870. This was before Brahms wrote his musical setting of *Ach, arme Welt*, in 1889, as the second of a set of three motets.

Strangely, he wrote the motets for the Hamburg Industrial Exhibition, and they were published in 1890. Set for four-part choir, with the usual soprano, alto, tenor, and bass lines, *Ach, arme Welt* is typical of Brahms's choral writing, rich in harmony, and indebted to Bach and Mendelssohn. The structure is strophic, that is, in verses, with repeated musical material used for different words. The effect of this briefest of Brahms's choral works is thus straightforward and relatively simple. Brahms wrote much of his music for choirs, and some of it is very complex and technically difficult.

Slightly antiquated and straightforward as the music may be, the text is more opaque. For von Laufenberg is not so much lamenting the negative state of the world as entreating us to draw inspiration and value from higher things. Underlying his apparently bleak approach to life is a passage from the Gospels: "Do not be afraid, little flock, for it is your Father's good pleasure to give you the kingdom. Sell your possessions, and give alms. Make purses for yourselves that do not wear out, an unfailing treasure in heaven, where no thief comes near and no moth destroys. For where your treasure is, there your heart will be also" (Luke 12:32–34). Once we recognize this, the final line of prayer in the text makes sense as a summary of the poet's attitude to life. Faith in the world, in wealth, or human accolade is false and futile. It all fades away in the face of inevitable and unavoidable death. For it is true that one never knows what is going to happen. For many people, this fact is a cue for disbelief, delusion, or indifference because many associate unpredictability with lack of control. We do not like to admit we are not in control, and rather than admit that God is in control, some people prefer to suppose that no one is, and that everything is either randomly determined, or can be controlled by those who try hard enough.

While this may seem depressing, von Laufenberg shows us that we do better to embrace the certainty of death, to rejoice in it and focus on the eternal. If, as Christ warns us, we hoard treasure on earth and put our security in it, we are bound to become distracted and ultimately disappointed. In our technological age, in which earning money and shopping are mutually dependent pastimes, it is so easy to be subsumed into consumer culture. Consumer culture turns goods into gods, and when we have made one purchase, we soon move on to the next. One day, there will not be a next purchase, and our life will be metaphorically, if not literally, over as the gods of our poor-in-spirit world abandon us. "All is vanity" (Ecclesiastes 1:2) teaches the Bible, and Jesus and von Laufenberg concur. Perhaps the realization of this spiritual and cosmological fact leads Brahms to keep his motet simple. An elaborate or lengthy setting, with counterpoint, repeated passages, wordplay, or clever musical fancies would have undermined the message of the text.

Yet there must be, and is, hope and cause for rejoicing. With von Laufenberg, we can seek to be freed from the burdens of the false world; to be released into a realm of being in which our treasure is heavenly and our hope eternal. It is not that we should refrain from shopping, nor enjoy the healthy delights of modern living, but if we can avoid dependency upon them, so that they do not become idols and gods, then we can live as spiritually aware, loving creatures of our heavenly Father. Then the pleasures of life become simple and straightforward. As we rejoice in the here and now, giving thanks for those whom we love and who love us, our perspective on life surely changes, and we realize that it is true that our treasure is where our heart is, and that if our heart is with God, happiness is his gift to us.

Lord, we are grateful for the world in which you have placed us and for the age in which we live. Help us not to become dependent on material things but to relish and enjoy the relationships with which you bless us, so that when our hour comes, we may have lived and loved well in anticipation of the heavenly treasure in which we rejoice here and now. Amen.

26. Traditional, arr. Parker • *Hark, I Hear the Harps Eternal*

CD Track 26—2:21

Hark, I hear the harps eternal
Ringing on the farther shore
As I near those swollen waters
With their deep and solemn roar.

Hallelujah, hallelujah, hallelujah, praise the lamb!
Hallelujah, hallelujah,
Glory to the great I AM!

And my soul, tho' stain'd with sorrow
Fading as the light of day,
Passes swiftly o'er those waters,
To the city far away.

Souls have cross'd before me, saintly,
To that land of perfect rest;
And I hear them singing faintly,
In the mansions of the blest.

Text: Traditional
Music: Traditional, arranged by Alice Parker (b. 1925)

Most of us, from time of time, wonder how and when we will die. Will I have an accident, be murdered, contract a disease, or fall asleep in my bed? Will I know of my death, so that I can prepare, or will it come like a thief in the night and catch me unawares? Some are utterly terrified of death, while others, perhaps nearing it, become reconciled to its inevitability and the relief from chronic or acute pain that it brings. Yet while every death is different, we are united by the fact of it, sharing its certainty with every other human being and animal, and even with our Lord Jesus Christ who himself passed through the doors of death before opening up the gates of glory three days later.

This song embodies the glory that accompanies death. Having its origin in the camp meetings of American spiritual revival, it was arranged by Alice Parker, a conductor and composer from Boston, Massachusetts, who has arranged many spiritual songs both in the black and white traditions. Her accomplished setting of this song of heavenly hope alternates between the major and minor modes, creating a to and fro effect that underscores the idea in the text of rowing a boat to the heavenly shore. The theology of the song is straightforward and orthodox: at death we set out on a brief but joyful journey, during which, while we cross profound depths, we have no cause to fear as we sing God's praise on our journey. In spite of the sins that blacken our name, God is merciful and will call us home to join with the saints who have gone before us, dwelling in those many mansions of which Jesus speaks: "In my Father's house there are many dwelling places. If it were not so, would I have told you that I go to prepare a place for you? And if I go and prepare a place for you, I will come again and will take you to myself, so that where I am, there you may be also. And you know the way to the place where I am going" (John 14:2–4). These are the words of eternal life and hope in which Christians can have confidence.

Yet there is always another side to death, and it would be foolish and dishonest to deny its reality. Since death is a necessary part of our existence, so too is grief, the experience of loss, pain, and regret that accompanies the death of a loved one. Most of us know what grief is even if we cannot satisfactorily describe it. Grief is what we feel when we know someone is dying. Grief is what we feel when we know that we are dying. And grief is, of course, what we feel when someone has gone. Grief is what we start with, and it never quite goes away.

While our grief never leaves us completely, as time goes by, we may begin to feel gratitude. Of course, we are not grateful that someone has died (although if our loved one has suffered terribly, we may experience some relief that their suffering has come to an end). The thankfulness we may feel as time goes by is gratitude to God, and to our loved ones, for all that they have been to us. In life it is other people, our friends and relations, who enrich us, teach us, support us, love us. This gives us cause to be grateful. And as time goes by, we become more and more grateful, for the time in which our loved ones were with us, and we learn to cherish the memories we have; to remember with a smile, to sigh, more and more with grateful contentment than with despair. To be able to do so is a gift, and the gift that another person is to us is not fully complete until we can handle our feelings and memories as things we have been given to hold, but only for a while. Thus as we learn to be grateful, we learn to hand our loved ones back to God, who gave us life, and who takes us back to himself at the end of our lives.

This is where God's glory comes in. The phrase "gone to glory" is very meaningful. The glory of God is something that we rarely notice, something that rarely strikes us. Yet, it is in times of grief and times of gratitude that God's glory is most apparent. God is the great "I am" (see Exodus 3:14), who created us and revealed himself to Moses, but his glory is also revealed in every human life: glory revealed at birth. The angels sang "Glory to God" when Jesus was born, but they could as well sing it when any one of us in born. For a human life is a living miracle.

Yet any human life is also finite. We are born to die, arriving in glory, and departing in glory, even if we are not always able to recognize it on either occasion. God's glory is reflected in our lives, and it is worth reflecting upon. Anyone who is born, or who dies (and that's all of us), is caught up in that wonderful, creative, pattern of love and hope and peace. Now and then, we may glimpse that glory, in the midst of gratitude, and even in grief.

God, our creator, in whose arms we die, give us a sense of your glory touching our lives, so that when our time comes, we may face death with courage and hope, secure in the promises of salvation you have made in Jesus Christ our Lord. Amen.

27. Copland • *Simple Gifts* from *Old American Songs*
CD Track 27—1:29

'Tis the gift to be simple, 'tis the gift to be free,
'Tis the gift to come down where you ought to be,
And when we find ourselves in the place just right,
'Twill be in the valley of love and delight.
When true simplicity is gained,
To bow and to bend we shan't be ashamed,
To turn, turn will be our delight,
Till by turning, turning we come round right.

Text: Joseph Brackett (1797–1882)
Music: Joseph Brackett, arranged by Aaron Copland (1900–1990)
and Irving Fine (1914–62)

Although the denomination of Christians known as Shakers began in Manchester, England, in the eighteenth century, they have become almost exclusively associated with New England in the United States. In 1774, Mother Ann Lee, the leader of what was then a nine-person group, moved everyone to New York City. Two years later, they settled in Niskayuna, New York. The community focused their spiritual lives on attaining holiness, which they felt was partly achieved by a spiritual process of ridding the body of sin by way of convulsions; this earned them the name *shaking Quakers*. For them the shaking engendered purification by the Holy Spirit. The Shakers lived in a celibate community, segregating men and women, who had different staircases in houses, and who sat on opposite sides of a room when together. Communities grew up in New England and elsewhere, and by the mid-nineteenth century, there were some 6,000 members in eighteen separate communities across eight states.

Shaker life was characterized by prayer and work. Women wore headscarves and men had ponytails. Shaker-style chairs were made with great care and skill, and with a philosophy not unlike a Benedictine approach: something well made is a form of prayer.

Worship took place in meetinghouses, where singing and music were very important, as were dancing, twitching, and shouting. While some of these practices caused consternation among their neighbors, the Shakers nevertheless produced many singable, delightful tunes, some of which used texts that drew on experiences of glossolalia (speaking in tongues): in Shaker theology, music could be a spiritual gift and was encouraged as such. One of the Shaker tunes, *Simple Gifts*, has become extremely famous, not only in its own right, but in how it has been used by other composers. Joseph Brackett, the original composer, was born in Cumberland, Maine, and joined the Shaker Community in Gorham, Maine. In 1819, he and his family moved with other Shakers to Poland Hill, Maine. He went on to serve as a leader in various Maine Shaker societies, and became an elder of the community of New Gloucester, Maine (now known as Sabbathday Lake, the last remaining Shaker community). He wrote *Simple Gifts* in 1848 while he was part of the community in Alfred, Maine.

Simple Gifts is not a hymn but a Shaker dance song. In the Shaker context, the distinction is straightforward: hymns have more than one verse. The last two lines of the single verse *Simple Gifts* refer to moves made in the dance, which obviously involved turning "again and again." The reference to bowing and bending may well have had an instructional purpose in terms of the way the music was danced. The song itself has traveled widely, most importantly through the work of Aaron Copland, who first used it at the end of his ballet *Appalachian Spring* of 1944, on which he collaborated with the choreographer Martha Graham (1894–1991). This ballet was very successful: he was awarded a Pulitzer Prize for it in 1945, and in the same year he made the music into an orchestral suite that has become even more popular. The ballet is ostensibly about a spring celebration of nineteenth-century American pioneers who have built a new farmhouse in Pennsylvania. The main characters include a newlywed couple and a revivalist preacher. It has nothing to do with the Appalachian Mountains!

On the other side of the Atlantic, *Simple Gifts* caught the attention of Sydney Carter (1915–2004), who worked for the British Council and BBC World Service. His hymn, known universally as *The Lord of the Dance*, written in 1966 is entirely based on the melody. Carter's adaptation is catchy, with words that tell the story of salvation, from nativity to Good Friday, beginning: "I danced in the morning when the world was begun." The refrain reminds us of the eternal dance of salvation: "Dance, then, wherever you may be; I am the Lord of the dance said he, And I'll lead you all, wherever you may be, And I'll lead you all in the dance, said he."

In the history of the church, the medium of dance has had a checkered history, during which it has often been alienated, proscribed, or at best ignored. Archbishop Thomas Cranmer's 1559 Prayer Book contained illustrations of the "Dance of Death" and Hans Holbein (c. 1465–1524) created a series of woodcut drawings in 1538 that include "The Alphabet of Death," in which each letter has a morbid theme. In another picture, "The New-Married Lady," the character of death insidiously dances before the bride and groom beating a tambourine. Old St. Paul's Cathedral, destroyed in the great London fire of 1666, had similarly macabre carvings lining the cloisters, illustrating sinister verses written by the poet John Lydgate, who was a contemporary of Chaucer. The idea of portraying the dance of death probably originated in France, where the earliest known depiction of such a dance was in the *Cimetière des Innocents* in Paris, painted in 1424, but later destroyed.

But Copland and Carter, following the Shaker tradition of *Simple Gifts*, point us toward a joyful spiritual dance, not of death but of resurrection life. For while the relationship between dance and faith has not always been a good one, liturgical dance is becoming more mainstream in worship, and the art form is at last gaining a position of respectability and value as an expression of faith. Indeed, it is the writer of Ecclesiastes who reminds us that: "For everything there is a season, and a time for every matter under heaven: . . . a time to weep, and a time to laugh; a time to mourn, and a time to dance . . ." (Ecclesiastes 3:1, 4).

Lord of the dance of life, give us the grace of simplicity as we move through our lives, that turning and turning around in love and delight, we may come around right, honoring you and following the footsteps of Christ. Amen.

28. Mozart • *Salus infirmorum* from *Litaniae Lauretanae*

CD Track 28—1:20

Salus infirmorum, refugiam peccatorum,
Consolatrix afflictorum, ora pro nobis.
Auxillium Christianorum, ora pro nobis.

Health of the frail, refuge of sinners,
Consoler of the afflicted, pray for us.
Help of Christians, pray for us.

Text: *Litaniae Laurentanae* (Lorettan Litany)
Music: Wolfgang Amadeus Mozart (1756–91) from
Litaniae Laurentanae K.109

Have you ever been ill? Of course you have! Mark Twain famously observed that death and taxes are the only two certainties in life, but I doubt that there is anyone alive who has never been ill at all. Illness is part of life, yet there is no more natural desire than to heal disease, and no more natural prayer than that for the sick.

In biblical times sickness and sin were connected. When Jesus meets a blind man his disciples ask him, "Who sinned, this man or his parents, that he was born blind?" (John 9:2). Jesus then denies that sin is the cause of the blindness. Nevertheless, the idea that sickness is the consequence of sin is still with us, and we find it lurking in this short petition from the Lorettan Litany. Many still believe that God would deliberately afflict someone as a kind of punishment, and so dismiss God as cruel. Yet our knowledge of biology assures us that what we call sickness is often a consequence of a natural process, and is therefore not the result of anything we say, think, or do. Conversely, some phenomena (such as sport, diet, or environment) can and do lead to injury or sickness, but it seems absurd to consider their consequences as judgments on those unfortunate enough to succumb to them.

People often wonder why God afflicts good people, but this is surely the wrong approach. Our cells mutate, other organisms seek to thrive even within our own bodies, and all of this happens as a consequence of the freedom that lies at the heart of all creation. The same biological processes that bring us to birth also contribute to both sudden and gradual change in our bodies. We ourselves are the location of constant change and decay. Thus, when it comes to healing, there is a useful sense in which it is better to think in terms of aligning our will to God, and seeking the inner healing that comes with an acceptance of our own frailty and mortality. James, in his epistle writes that "the prayer of faith will save the sick, and the Lord will raise them up; and anyone who has committed sins will be forgiven" (James 5:15). The truth of this lies not merely in occasional miraculous healings that may be encountered, but in the everyday remissions and reliefs that God grants to those who truly rest upon his all-creating, merciful love.

Music can have great healing power, and its therapeutic value is widely attested to by professionals who use it with those for whom other forms of communication or relaxation have made no headway. As there is not much music employing texts that speak of healing, Mozart's Lorettan Litany, written for use in Salzburg Cathedral in May 1771, is therefore quite unusual. Intended to aid private devotion, and employing texts used in liturgies of pilgrimage to the Italian town of Loreto, we find within it this gem of a prayer, directed to the Virgin, seeking healing for those who, whether through sin or not, are in need of physical and spiritual healing. As we all suffer from illness at some time, and are all sinners, this prayer has a universality to which we can all relate, even if we are not in the habit of seeking the Virgin's assistance in such intercession.

Mozart's brief setting of this text has two distinct parts: a slow main section in which the first two lines of the text are articulated in a rather ponderous, dolorous way, rather like a sick person moving aimlessly about. Then follows a final, jauntier, upbeat section in which the third line is given impetus as hope springs eternal and the musical conclusion is reached. While there does not seem to be any specific textual reason for the division of the brief text in this way, musically it is very Mozartian, and this archetypically classical approach presents a musical question and answerlike structure, even within such a short span of time.

In music, the word *classical* is often used as a generic term to categorize Western art music, but strictly speaking, the term should be used in relation to the music of composers such as Mozart, Haydn, and Beethoven, whose compositions embodied a particular aesthetic by which dissonance, harmony, and musical structure combine and compete in a way that engenders tension and resolution in exquisite balance. In classical music, there is invariably a solution to the dilemmas posed within the melody and harmony of the music, but the journey toward it, navigated by geniuses such as Mozart, leaves us amazed and enchanted. Thus classical style can be inherently comic, when, as with a joke, there is a punch line at the end. By the same token, classical music can portray pain and wounding, in the certainty that there will be ultimate healing when after tonal "bruisings" and harmonic wanderings, melodies return and chords resolve. For this reason many still find music of the classical period so satisfying, for it eventually takes you where you both expect and want to go. Classical music is suited to prayer for healing: for in Mozart's brief movement we get a result so that at the end, all is well. So it is with our prayer: our prayers for healing are answered, not according to our will, but according to God's will, and while we may not know the discordant journeys of sickness that any of us must take, we know that in Christ's healing hands there is always resolution as we are restored to wholeness and harmony in life, or in death.

Father of all, have mercy on all who call on you in the pain of sickness, injury, or grief. Comfort them with the promise of eternal wholeness, and if it be your will, grant them physical renewal and regeneration until that day when you call us into your everlasting arms, for the sake of Jesus Christ, our healer and friend. Amen.

29. Argento • *Let All the World*
CD Track 30—3:22

Let all the world in every corner sing,
My God and King!
The heavens are not too high,
His praise may thither fly;
The earth is not too low,
His praises there may grow.
Let all the world in every corner sing,
My God and King!

Let all the world in every corner sing,
My God and King!
The Church with psalms must shout,
No door can keep them out;
But above all, the heart
Must bear the longest part.
Let all the world in every corner sing,
My God and King!

Text: George Herbert (1593–1633)
Music: Dominick Argento (b. 1927)

These words of encouragement and praise come from the pen
of George Herbert, who was one of England's greatest poets,
and whose piety and pastoral ministry have served as an example
to countless clergy and laity for the past four centuries. His most
famous set of poems, entitled *The Temple*, includes the hymn *Let All
the World*. Containing 160 poems, it was published posthumously
by his friend Nicholas Ferrar (1592–1637). Herbert sent them
to Ferrar at the very end of his life, and suggested that if Ferrar

thought them valueless, they should be burned. Herbert's modesty was ill-placed, and he is now revered as something close to a saint by English-speaking Christians.

He was related to the family of the Earl of Pembroke, and was born in Wales, in Montgomery Castle. His father died when Herbert was three, and his mother Magdalen was a good friend of John Donne (1571–1631), the famous poet and dean of St. Paul's. At age ten, Herbert went to Westminster School, where he was influenced by the Dean of Westminster, Launcelot Andrewes, one of the great thinkers and preachers of his day. In 1609, Herbert went to Trinity College, Cambridge, where he spent twenty years as student, college fellow, and university orator. In 1623, he was elected a Member of Parliament for Montgomery. Sometime around 1625, Herbert was ordained deacon, and became a Prebendary of Lincoln Cathedral, and he moved to Leighton Bromswold. In 1630, he moved to Fugglestone-with-Bemerton in Wiltshire. Herbert only lived another three years, but in this time he gained a reputation as something of a saint within the villages, and he wrote much poetry, and a book on rural ministry entitled *A Priest to the Temple*, or *The Country Parson, His Character and Rule of Life*. That book is still highly respected today, not only as a description of early seventeenth-century ecclesiastical life, but as a manual of pastoral care.

Let All the World, along with *Teach Me My God and King* and *King of Glory, King of Peace*, are among Herbert's most famous poems. It was written as a hymn, with the phrase "Let all the world in every corner sing, My God and King!" serving as an antiphon, flanking the two brief verses. It is often sung as a hymn today, with the tune *Luckington* composed by Basil Harwood (1859–1949). It also is featured as the finale to Ralph Vaughan Williams's setting of *Five Mystical Songs*: five poems by Herbert. It is not surprising that a text that extols the virtues of worldwide singing should attract composers, and more recently, the American composer Dominick Argento has contributed a version to the repertoire. Better known for his thirteen operas, Argento won the Pulitzer Prize in 1975 for a song cycle, *From the Diary of Virginia Woolf*. His brief but confident anthem, *Let All the World* was composed in 1980 and is subtitled *A Festive Hymn for Chorus*, requiring brass quartet, timpani, and organ to join with the choir.

The piece opens with stately brass motifs and solemn drum beats ushering in an arching melody. The drum cadences continue throughout, punctuating the music, as we are carried on a regal journey through the text, reminiscent of the funeral music of Purcell and the choral music of Parry and Vaughan Williams. Argento does not make his anthem exuberant or brash, as he might have done, but prefers a more sedate, dignified approach, giving the text a gravitas that balances the universal appeal to praise God in every corner of the world. Although Argento's is a serious-minded setting, it is no less accessible, and a live performance in a large acoustic may produce spine-tingling results as the music echoes around. Argento once said that music "began as an emotional language. For me, all music begins where speech stops," and this anthem certainly speaks to us on a level of rhythm and harmony that transcends the straightforward message of the words. In a sense his description of music is universal: the sonorities of harmony and melody add dimensions to the experience that the poetry alone cannot deliver.

Some people say that good poetry makes for bad music, and that the best songs have mediocre texts. It is a popular but unfounded prejudice, but it is based on the belief that really good poetry does not need music to make it sing. George Herbert's poetry is undoubtedly very fine, as well as being spiritually authentic, and so it is a rare musician who can enhance it. Yet, for all its pomp and color, Herbert's text embodies a profound spiritual truth. At the end of the second stanza, he declares, "But above all, the heart must bear the longest part," and what he means is that in spite of hymns and praises, there must be the inner commitment, a heartfelt conviction, and desire to worship God. Singing God's praise is all very well, but one must mean it too. This is even more relevant today than it was for Herbert, who was writing at a time when hymn singing was nowhere near as widespread as it is now. There are thousands of hymns to sing nowadays, and much other sacred music besides, but when we sing hymns or listen to them, our calling is to make them our own. Hymns and anthems are often prayers, or statements of faith, or invocations to praise God. As we listen to them with the ears of faith, let us also pray through them, to our God, who hears and answers prayer as it is offered in every corner of the world.

God, our king, you let all the world sing your praise, and you are worthy of all glory and honor. By your Spirit, enable the music of our hearts to fly heavenward, to play even a small part in the great harmony of worship offered before your eternal throne. Amen.

30. Vaughan Williams • *O Clap Your Hands*
CD Track 29—3:24

O clap your hands, all ye people: shout unto God with the
voice of triumph.
For the LORD most high is terrible: He is a great King over
all the earth. . . .
God is gone up with a shout, the LORD with the sound of
a trumpet.
Sing praises to God, . . . sing praises unto our King, . . .
For God is the King of all the earth: sing ye praises with
understanding.
God reigneth over the heathen, God sitteth upon the throne
of his holiness.
Sing ye praises unto our King, sing praises!

Text: Psalm 47:1–2, 5–8 (KJV)
Music: Ralph Vaughan Williams (1872–1958)

While this text, and Vaughan Williams's majestic setting of
it, is often associated with Ascensiontide, there is no need
to confine its use to that season. The psalmist did not have Jesus'
ascension in mind when he wrote, "God is gone up," even if he did
have a vision of God enthroned in glory, perhaps as Isaiah did: 'I
saw the Lord sitting on a throne, high and lofty; and the hem of his
robe filled the temple. Seraphs were in attendance above him; each
had six wings: with two they covered their faces, and with two they
covered their feet, and with two they flew'" (Isaiah 6:1–2).

The psalmist had in mind the excitement and delight of some
kind of enthronement of God as king. Many scholars have concluded
that this psalm, along with Psalms 93 and 95–99, were written
for and used at an annual festival that emphasized and worshiped

Jahweh as King of Creation. Such a celebration would have been uplifting in every sense of the word, the name of God would be raised and praised, but the effect on the congregation would have been inspiring and unifying. The reference to the trumpet brings to mind a description of such an event when King David brought the ark of the covenant into the city amid great rejoicing, singing, and dancing: "So David and all the house of Israel brought up the ark of the LORD with shouting, and with the sound of the trumpet" (2 Samuel 6:15).

The great English folk-song collector, hymnologist, and composer Ralph Vaughan Williams was no stranger to coronations: his splendid arrangement of *All People That on Earth Do Dwell* ("The Old Hundredth") was composed for Queen Elizabeth II's Coronation in 1953. *O Clap Your Hands* would make a good coronation anthem, but has not yet been used as such. Written in 1920, at the beginning of his tenure as musical director of London's renowned Bach Choir, *O Clap Your Hands* is a sort of fanfare for his musical career, which really began around that time, and saw him world-famous by the end of the decade. He had been writing significant works since the beginning of the century, but the 1920s marked a real turning point. The war of 1914–18 clearly affected Vaughan Williams's faith, but he continued to write sacred music, including his beautifully archaic Mass setting of 1920–21.

O Clap Your Hands opens with a motif sounded on the trumpet (in the original organ and brass version), which motif forms the basis of all that follows. A quieter central section creates tension as the choir begins a slow crescendo to the final line. Rather than simply set the text as a rambunctious yell, Vaughan Williams tones down the exuberance in order to create a steady buildup, with suppressed joy, eventually opening out at the end, rather like a sunrise or flower blooming. The direction of the piece is thus constantly upward, a steady climb, tonally and emotionally.

Nowadays many are wary of hand clapping in the context of worship, and where people do clap their hands in praise, it tends not to be when music by composers such as Vaughan Williams is sung. Established, classical choral music might sing about handclapping, but perish the thought that anyone might actually do it! Even applause in church is frowned upon in some places. In the Bible, the clapping of hands is a little ambiguous: sometimes it indicated disaster, rather than joy: "Clap your hands and stamp your foot, and say, Alas for all the vile abominations of the house of Israel! For they shall fall by the sword, by famine, and by pestilence" (Ezekiel 6:11). What we take for granted as a sign of appreciation was not always so, although in Psalm 47 the clapping clearly is joyful, just as it is in Isaiah: "For you shall go out in joy, and be led back in peace; the mountains and the hills before you shall burst into song, and all the trees of the field shall clap their hands" (Isaiah 55:12).

The expression of such joy that is rather self-consciously shown by appreciative applause is the same delight that makes children clap their hands with glee, unprompted. It is extremely unlikely that someone once wondered, *what is the best way to show and express pleasure—I know, let's hit our hands together*, but rather that this primitive expressive act has been civilized into formal applause. Worship can also become too formal, and the expression of godly emotion, too wooden. Some styles of worship are much more at home with spontaneity, clapping and other joyful expressions of adoration and delight. It may seem a long way from the world of Vaughan Williams, Mozart, and Palestrina, but freer forms of expression are nonetheless authentic, and it can be far too easy to forget that the authors of these biblical texts, especially the psalms, may well have had such exuberance in mind, before serious-minded composers set their words for rendition by highly skilled but fairly straight-laced singers and musicians schooled in the Western tradition. It may well be that we delight in the beauty, the precision, the gravitas of much choral music, and so we should, but let us never forget that our calling, in praise, is to clap our hands and sing praises to God our king, who reigns over all the earth!

God above, you reign over heaven and earth, and although you command a terrible power, your nature is righteousness, mercy, and love. May we always be inspired to celebrate your salvation, wrought in Jesus, by sounding instruments and singing your praises, until that day when, in unison with heavenly choirs and angels' trumpets, we may clap our hands for joy in your eternal kingdom. Amen.

A FOUR-SESSION
GROUP STUDY
of

O CLAP
YOUR
HANDS

Introduction to the Four-Session Group Study

I f and when several people in a church or choir are reading this book simultaneously at home, it can be edifying and inspiring to meet together (probably weekly, or perhaps monthly) to share impressions, responses, and wider thoughts that your reading and listening has yielded. Some reactions may be gentle and comforting, or they may be strong, even negative. In any event it is good to share with others, and these sets of discussion questions and activities are offered to facilitate such gatherings of folk who have read and listened to at least some of the material before meeting.

At the beginning of the book there are some suggestions for how to use it with a small group, in a devotional way. A study group is different, and it is not recommended that you combine both approaches on the same occasion. However, any study group should open and conclude with prayer, for the meeting itself is a form of fellowship and should be conducted as such.

It should never be assumed that such a group can be made up only of practicing musicians, for while insights into performance may be helpful, they can be distracting, and ultimately it is what we hear through our ears that enters our souls and touches our hearts. The presence in a group of those who are not so musical may be of great benefit to those who are, for no one will be able to hide behind jargon or received opinion! It is also good for nonmusicians to hear what musicians experience when they play or sing. In this way it is hoped that the study material can be beneficial to all-comers. The only instrument required is a CD player.

No one should be criticized for their opinions or responses, and care should be taken when topics move into areas of pastoral concern, particularly in the final session. It may be appropriate to agree to confidentiality boundaries within a group, and follow-up counseling should be available from a minister.

Generally, this discussion material is offered in the hope that it will enable individuals to get more from the book by sharing responses and ideas, and to be led in new ways together on their journey of faith.

Session One • Opening Our Lips

Begin with a prayer and then listen to Viadana's *Exsultate, justi*, track #1. What do you think of it? Do you like this kind of music? Why? Or why not? What preconceptions do you bring to this music? What are you expecting from this book and from discussions around its chapters? Share some of your initial thoughts. Also introduce yourselves if the group members are not familiar with one another.

Consider some of the themes of the Introduction: are you involved in chamber music? If anyone is, perhaps they can explain what it is like to make music on that scale. Continue to reflect on how the way in which we play music is like life and how it might mirror the life of faith. Be creative together in your thinking and do not be shy with your thoughts. If you are not a musician, think perhaps of other activities, such as painting, cooking, or gardening. What are we doing to, for, and with God's creation when we work with plants, colors, foods, or sounds? What would life be like if we could not, or did not?

Listen to Rachmaninov's *Bogoroditse Devo*, track #4. Can you imagine anything more beautiful? What a gift it must be to invent such sounds and to be able to produce them! Reflect on the effort and skill required. What is talent, and in what sense does it come from God? If it doesn't come from God, where might it come from (even if you don't agree with this possibility, imagine you do and try to make a case). How does science explain music? Is there more to it than that?

Read 1 Corinthians 12. What are your gifts? Do you feel as a group that God's gifts are shared among you? Do you wish you had other, more, or different gifts?

What are your experiences of speaking in tongues (glossolalia) and what do you think about it? Is music a "tongue" that might be understood or interpreted? Is music a spiritual gift? How do you feel about suggesting it is when Paul does not mention it? How literally do we have to treat his words? Can they mean more than he says, or less, or something different? How comparable is the Corinthian pagan situation to our day? Do we live in a pagan age in which music is expressive of and servant to values Christians abhor?

Listen to *Psalm 150*, track #6, sung in plainsong. This the most ancient form of music we have. How is it that it speaks today? What values of a thousand years ago do we still hold dear? Have we progressed, or are we basically the same, such that Paul's letters are as relevant today as 2,000 years ago?

Is it the same with music? Do pieces mean the same now as they did when originally written? Should we play them as such? What does it mean to be authentic; to seek to recreate and live in the past, or is that fundamentally impossible and therefore futile? Should an old piece be made to adapt to keep its relevance to today? Is this also true of our worship and faith?

Conclude by listening to Kedrov's *Otche nash*, track #5, and saying the Lord's Prayer together.

Session Two • Music, Mercy, and the Mass

L isten to the *Kyrie* from Langlais's *Messe Solennelle*, track #8. Why is there a plea for mercy at the beginning of the Eucharist? Does Langlais convey the right mood? Does the music convey a proper sense of mystery, guilt, shame, awe, or fear, and does it remind us that while we seek forgiveness we also have assurance of mercy? Do you feel like a sinner? Why do we seek mercy if we have already been granted it? Do you ever feel that you haven't been forgiven by God? Why might that be?

Do you ever feel that you are forgiven, and if so what does that feel like?

Compare the appeal for forgiveness in Langlais's Mass, with that of Palestrina's *Miserere*, track #15. Can you describe any differences between the two?

Read the account of Jesus' triumphal entry into Jerusalem (Luke 19:28–40). Listen to Monteverdi's setting of the *Benedictus*, track #12. How does the use of this text in the middle of the Eucharist strike you? Sometimes it is omitted. Is it used in your church, and why is it used (or not)? Should it be sung or not?

Listen to Esquivel's *Ego sum panis vivus*, track #14. Many non-churchgoers do not have a grasp of what the Eucharist is about. Imagine that you have to explain what Communion is, using this piece as a starting point. How easy is it? Does music help explain things? How, or why not?

Listen to the *Agnus Dei* by Rheinberger, track #13. What is the textual connection between the Kyrie and Agnus Dei? Does Rheinberger's music strike you as authentic? Does he believe in forgiveness? Can you hear it in the music? How do you reach an answer?

Finally, if there is time, have a general discussion about the merits of Mass settings you use in your parish or church. What makes a setting good? Should the Eucharist always have music?

Session Three • Musical Seasoning

Recap some of the material of the previous two sessions. What liturgical season are we currently in? Why are you studying this course now, rather than at any other time?

How seasonal is your church? Does the liturgy follow different liturgical seasons? Are the colors varied for different times of year and is there a different feel to the hymns and other music? Are there times when *alleluia* is not said or sung?

Listen to the creed from Thomson's *Mass*, track #10. Do you like it? Is it seasonal? Are there some times for saying the creed and times for not doing so? When should the creed be said or sung? How often does your church use it and when did you last say the creed? Do you think you should say the creed more or less often? What is the point of saying or singing the creed?

Without consulting any books or people, write down the seasons and festivals of the liturgical year, commencing with Advent. Then compare notes and see how complete a picture you get. (Someone in the group will need a cycle of prayer or lectionary against which to compare the results.)

What difference, if any, does music make to a liturgical season? Can it set the tone of a season? Listen to these works in this order, with little break between: Handl's *Rorate caeli*, track #16; Lotti's *Crucifixus*, track #19; Byrd's *Terra tremuit*, track #21; Mendelssohn's *Am Himmelfahrtstage*, track #22. Can you identify the seasons, and do you feel there is a progression from one to the other? Discuss your responses and impressions.

Finish by saying the creed together.

Session Four • Heaven and Healing

Begin by listening to Sowerby's *Eternal Light*, track #24. Do you like it? Why?

Alcuin's prayer is very ancient and Sowerby's music quite modern. Do they go well together? Can you say why? In that marriage, does the age gap matter? Does knowing that this music is American make any difference to your appreciation of it?

Listen to Ives's *Psalm 100*, track #7. Can you hear any similarities between the works of these two composers? Did you expect to? Does a country have a certain style of music that can be detected, or should music transcend race, creed, or gender? Is the same true of spirituality? Is sacred music any different from secular music?

What about *Simple Gifts*, track #27? Listen to it, perhaps a couple of times, join in and sing along. Share any experiences of this kind of music that you may already have. Is it too primitive or simple? Do you prefer more sophisticated offerings? What might God think?

Now try *Hark, I Hear the Harps Eternal*, track #26. Is it possible not to like this exuberant song? What does it make you feel about death? Can or should one really feel like this? Are we expected to take an unrealistic approach to dying? Perhaps share some thoughts about dying (but be sensitive to others who may be recently bereaved). What music would you like at your funeral, and why?

To end on a less morbid note, many people are involved in music therapy, and attest to its efficacy. Listen to Mozart's *Salus infirmorum*, track #28: can music have healing power? How does music speak to and touch us, and where is God in such a phenomenon?

Finally, turn back to the poem by George Herbert at the beginning of the book. Do you understand it? Is it right to thank church music, or God, for its beauties? Compare it with *Let All the World*, track #29, and consider the journey this book has taken:

have you enjoyed the journey? Are you interested in thanking God for the gift of music? If you are, do so in prayer and then finish by listening to either O *Clap Your Hands*, track #30, by Vaughan Williams or Argento's *Let All the World*, track #29.

Acknowledgments

It was my good fortune in the summer of 2007 to have a study leave, during which time I was able to travel and write. In June, I was extremely fortunate and blessed to be welcomed by the Community of Jesus in Orleans, Massachusetts, the church home of the choir Gloriæ Dei Cantores. During my stay this book was conceived, so I acknowledge a debt of gratitude (and hospitality) to all those in the Community and at Paraclete Press with whom I enjoyed talking. This book is my "thank you" to these people for their generosity and the friendship I encountered.

I also wish to thank those in England who gave me space and time to write this book upon my return. Bishop Peter Wheatley and Fr. Richard Knowling made my sabbatical possible in the first place, and the Reverends Jackie Fish, Barry Oakley, and Reg Dunn looked after the parish of St. Mary Magdalene, Enfield, while I was away.

Most of all, and not for the first time, I want to thank my wife, Jessica, and my three-year-old daughter, Maria, who were left to fend for themselves, sometimes even when I was at home writing! Jessica and I share a love of church music and of singing it; my prayer for Maria, enshrined in this book, is that she will grow up to do the same.

Where to Obtain the Gloriæ Dei Cantores Recordings Used in This Book

Masters of the Renaissance
ISBN: 978-1-55725-497-9, $16.95

1. Viadana • *Exsultate, justi*
11. Lassus • *Sanctus* from *Missa Super Bella Amfitrit' Altera*
14. Esquivel • *Ego sum panis vivus*
16. Handl • *Rorate caeli*
17. Hassler • *Dixit Maria*
18. Nanino • *Adoramus te, Christe*
21. Byrd • *Terra tremuit*
23. Philips • *Tibi laus*

"Truly golden sound and beautifully nuanced singing.
Sacred illumination is their mission,
and they achieve it with sincerity and power."
—*American Record Guide*

Edmund Rubbra: The Sacred Muse
ISBN: 978-1-55725-194-7, $16.95

2. Rubbra • *Nunc Dimittis in A flat*

"Particularly deserving of serious attention,
and invites numerous listenings.
This is an essential disc."
—*Classics Today*

Thou Art My Refuge:
Psalms of Salvation and Mercy
ISBN: 978-1-55725-451-1, $16.95

3. Hylton Stewart • *Psalm 137*

"Thanks to the superb efforts of this very sensitive,
responsive choir, its knowing director, and a pair of
first-rate organists, we experience something of the
uniquely expressive power inherent
in this manner of psalm-singing."
—*Classics Today*

Sacred Songs of Russia
ISBN: 978-1-55725-224-1, $16.95

4. Rachmaninov • *Bogoroditse Devo*
5. Kedrov • *Otche nash (Our Father)*
20. Tchaikovsky • *Angel vopiyáshe*

"This is the best—the best—compilation of standard
Russian sacred choral music."
—*American Record Guide*

Esperanza
The Gift of Spanish Song
ISBN: 978-1-55725-367-5, $16.95

6. Gregorian Chant • *Psalm 150*

"Rendered with exquisite reverence."—*Fanfare*

The Lord Is My Shepherd
American Psalmody Vol. III
ISBN: 978-1-55725-275-3, $16.95

7. Ives • *Psalm 100*

"While the individual pieces are unified by a deep
spirituality and a strong engagement with their
texts, the range of their soundscapes is impressive."
—*Classical Music Review*

Eclipse
The Voice of Jean Langlais
ISBN: 978-1-55725-545-7, $29.95

8. Langlais • *Kyrie* from *Messe Solennelle*

"The *Messe Solennelle* is absolutely magnificent . . .
the perfect tempi in a beautiful acoustic.
I should say, one of the very best performances
of this mass I have ever heard."
—Marie-Louise Langlais

The Doctrine of Wisdom
Sacred Choral Music of William Mathias
ISBN: 978-1-55725-210-4, $16.95

9. Mathias • *Gloria* from *Missa Brevis*

"Beautiful, affecting music."—*Chicago Tribune*

Aaron Copland & Virgil Thomson
Sacred and Secular Choral Music
ISBN: 978-1-55725-274-6, $16.95

10. Thomson • *Credo* from *Mass for Two-Part Chorus and Percussion*
27. Copland • *Simple Gifts* from *Old American Songs*

"The excellent Gloriæ Dei Cantores choir . . . faithfully deliver the music with enthusiasm and solid technique."
—*Classics Today*

Josef Gabriel Rheinberger
Motets, Masses & Hymns
ISBN: 978-1-55725-251-7, $16.95

13. Rheinberger • *Agnus Dei* from *Mass in E flat*

"Excellent performances by Gloriæ Dei Cantores, whose full-bodied yet carefully balanced ensemble sound is perfect for these 'romantic' works."
—*Classics Today*

Giovanni Pierluigi da Palestrina
ISBN: 978-1-55725-240-1, $16.95

15. Palestrina • *Miserere nostri, Domine*

"Patterson clearly has genius in selecting just the right tempos and dynamics . . . serious, winning and convincing. If we have ever had a finer Palestrina recording available, I've not heard it."
—*In Tune*

Paths of Grace
ISBN: 978-1-55725-517-4, $12.99

19. Lotti • *Crucifixus*

"An unalloyed delight . . . fully on par with the best choral ensembles recording today."
—*Fanfare*

Mendelssohn & Brahms
Sacred Motets
ISBN: 978-1-55725-243-2, $16.95

22. Mendelssohn • *Am Himmelfahrtstage*
25. Brahms • *Ach, arme Welt*

> "I doubt that Brahms himself could have imagined a more perfect performance. . . . Balance, ensemble, and intonation are perfect, as one has come to expect of the Cantores. Enough with superlatives; add this disc to your collection."
> —*The American Organist*

Eternal Light
ISBN: 978-1-55725-435-1, $12.99

24. Sowerby • *Eternal Light*

> "The moment I pushed the start button for this one, I melted into a happy trance. When I 'came to' about an hour later, I was surer than ever that the fabulous singers of Gloriæ Dei Cantores make up America's very finest amateur choir. . . . I've never heard such rapt and fathomless spiritual intensity from anybody else."
> —*American Record Guide*

Appalachian Sketches
ISBN: 978-1-55725-281-4, $16.95

26. Traditional, arr. Parker • *Hark, I Hear the Harps Eternal*

> "Director Elizabeth Patterson always is careful to honor the music's historical context and—most importantly—the words. And we hear every one, delivered with conviction and concern for balance among sections and overall ensemble blend."
> —*Classics Today*

Mozart
Rare Choral Works
ISBN: 978-1-55725-479-5, $29.95

28. Mozart • *Salus infirmorum* from *Litaniae Lauretanae*

"The performances are very good, especially the finely executed, energetic, vibrant choral singing and the equally dynamic and tightly-knit orchestra accompaniment."
—*Classics Today*

Prism
The Choral Artistry of Gloriæ Dei Cantores
ISBN: 978-1-55725-350-7, $12.99

29. Argento • *Let All the World*

"Emotional intensity and aching spirituality."
—*American Record Guide*

Joy and Gladness
ISBN: 978-1-55725-492-4, $12.99

30. Vaughan Williams • *O Clap Your Hands*

"Whether singing a cappella or accompanied by keyboard and brass instruments, the 40-voice ensemble produces a robust choral tone that is enhanced by reverberant acoustics."
—*Cleveland Plain Dealer*

These recordings are available from most booksellers or through Paraclete Press:

www.paracletepress.com • 1-800-451-5006.
Try your local bookstore first.

Credits for the compact disc accompanying O Clap Your Hands:
The dynamic range of this recording has been digitally enhanced to provide a more pleasurable listening experience. / Producers: Elizabeth C. Patterson, Dr. Craig Timberlake, Richard K. Pugsley, Irina Riazanova, James Litton / Musical Consultants: Dr. Craig Timberlake, Peter Jermihov / Recording Engineers: Joseph Chilorio, Steve Colby, Scott Kent / Contains previously released material recorded at Mechanics Hall, Worcester, MA; Methuen Memorial Music Hall, Methuen, MA; Church of the Transfiguration, Orleans, MA / ©℗ 2008 Gloriæ Dei Artes Foundation, Inc. / Originally released 1989–2007. All rights reserved. Total running time 77:12.

About Paraclete Press

Who We Are

Paraclete Press is an ecumenical publisher of books and recordings on Christian spirituality. Our publishing represents a full expression of Christian belief and practice—from Catholic to Evangelical, from Protestant to Orthodox.

Paraclete Press is the publishing arm of the Community of Jesus, an ecumenical monastic community in the Benedictine tradition. As such, we are uniquely positioned in the marketplace without connection to a large corporation and with informal relationships to many branches and denominations of faith.

We like it best when people buy our books from booksellers, our partners in successfully reaching as wide an audience as possible.

What We Are Doing

Books • Paraclete Press publishes books that show the richness and depth of what it means to be Christian. Although Benedictine spirituality is at the heart of all that we do, we publish books that reflect the Christian experience across many cultures, time periods, and houses of worship.

We publish books that nourish the vibrant life of the church and its people—books about spiritual practice, formation, history, ideas, and customs.

We have several different series of books within Paraclete Press, including the best-selling Living Library series of modernized classic texts; A Voice from the Monastery—giving voice to men and women monastics about what it means to live a spiritual life today; award-winning literary faith fiction; and books that explore Judaism and Islam and discover how these faiths inform Christian thought and practice.

Recordings • From Gregorian chant to contemporary American choral works, our music recordings celebrate the richness of sacred choral music through the centuries. Paraclete is proud to distribute the recordings of the internationally acclaimed choir Gloriæ Dei Cantores, who have been praised for their "rapt and fathomless spiritual intensity" by *American Record Guide,* and the Gloriæ Dei Cantores Schola, which specializes in the study and performance of Gregorian chant. Paraclete is also the exclusive North American distributor of the recordings of the Monastic Choir of St. Peter's Abbey in Solesmes, France, long considered to be a leading authority on Gregorian chant performance.

Learn more about us at our Web site:

www.paracletepress.com,
or call us toll-free at 1-800-451-5006.

Also Available from Paraclete Press

O Come Emmanuel
Gordon Giles

ISBN: 978-1-55725-515-0
176 pages | $14.95
Paperback

Make Christmas special this year by exploring the legends, message, and theology behind some of your favorite carols and hymns. This book of daily devotions will take you from December 1 to January 6, from the first days of Advent, through Christmas, ending at Epiphany. Each day, Gordon Giles invites you to draw closer to God through spiritual and historical explorations of beloved, familiar music.

The Song of Prayer
Community of Jesus

ISBN: 978-1-55725-576-1
112 pages | $19.95
Paperback with instructional CD

Pray with your whole self—using body, spirit, and mind—just as ancient and medieval Christians once did. You don't have to be highly musical in order to get started. This complete guide to the practice of Gregorian chant shows curious individuals as well as study groups in churches and classrooms the basics of chant, with some preliminary instruction in Latin, chant notation, its history and development, and theology. An instructional 45-minute CD accompanies the book, and provides examples of each chant, making learning easy and practical.

Kaleidoscope

Gloriæ Dei Cantores

ISBN: 978-1-55725-542-6, $16.95, CD

C elebrate the sacred sounds of America with *Kaleidoscope*. This is the music that has lofted through church rafters across the United States since its founding, and continues to bring comfort and strength to its faithful people today. Features a new arrangement of "Amazing Grace"; classics by some of America's great composers such as Aaron Copland, Virgil Thomson, Leo Sowerby, and Paul Manz; and beloved hymns from Appalachia and the South, arranged by Alice Parker and others. Also features the brass quintet Gabriel V in a new arrangement of the spiritual "Let Us Break Bread Together."

These recordings are available from most booksellers or through Paraclete Press:

www.paracletepress.com • **1-800-451-5006**.

Try your local bookstore first.